Wendi Heinzelman

Resource Management Policies for Wireless and Visual Sensor Networks

Stanislava Soro
Wendi Heinzelman

Resource Management Policies for Wireless and Visual Sensor Networks

VDM Verlag Dr. Müller

Impressum/Imprint (nur für Deutschland/ only for Germany)
Bibliografische Information der Deutschen Nationalbibliothek: Die Deutsche Nationalbibliothek
verzeichnet diese Publikation in der Deutschen Nationalbibliografie; detaillierte bibliografische
Daten sind im Internet über http://dnb.d-nb.de abrufbar.
Alle in diesem Buch genannten Marken und Produktnamen unterliegen warenzeichen-, marken-
oder patentrechtlichem Schutz bzw. sind Warenzeichen oder eingetragene Warenzeichen der
jeweiligen Inhaber. Die Wiedergabe von Marken, Produktnamen, Gebrauchsnamen,
Handelsnamen, Warenbezeichnungen u.s.w. in diesem Werk berechtigt auch ohne besondere
Kennzeichnung nicht zu der Annahme, dass solche Namen im Sinne der Warenzeichen- und
Markenschutzgesetzgebung als frei zu betrachten wären und daher von jedermann benutzt
werden dürften.

Coverbild: www.purestockx.com

Verlag: VDM Verlag Dr. Müller Aktiengesellschaft & Co. KG
Dudweiler Landstr. 99, 66123 Saarbrücken, Deutschland
Telefon +49 681 9100-698, Telefax +49 681 9100-988, Email: info@vdm-verlag.de
Zugl.: Rochester NY, University of Rochester, Ph.D. Diss., 2007

Herstellung in Deutschland:
Schaltungsdienst Lange o.H.G., Berlin
Books on Demand GmbH, Norderstedt
Reha GmbH, Saarbrücken
Amazon Distribution GmbH, Leipzig
ISBN: 978-3-639-10915-3

Imprint (only for USA, GB)
Bibliographic information published by the Deutsche Nationalbibliothek: The Deutsche
Nationalbibliothek lists this publication in the Deutsche Nationalbibliografie; detailed
bibliographic data are available in the Internet at http://dnb.d-nb.de.
Any brand names and product names mentioned in this book are subject to trademark, brand or
patent protection and are trademarks or registered trademarks of their respective holders. The
use of brand names, product names, common names, trade names, product descriptions etc.
even without a particular marking in this works is in no way to be construed to mean that such
names may be regarded as unrestricted in respect of trademark and brand protection legislation
and could thus be used by anyone.

Cover image: www.purestockx.com

Publisher:
VDM Verlag Dr. Müller Aktiengesellschaft & Co. KG
Dudweiler Landstr. 99, 66123 Saarbrücken, Germany
Phone +49 681 9100-698, Fax +49 681 9100-988, Email: info@vdm-publishing.com

Printed in the U.S.A.
Printed in the U.K. by (see last page)
ISBN: 978-3-639-10915-3

To our families.

Contents

List of Tables

List of Figures

Chapter 1

Introduction

Wireless Sensor Networks have a tremendous potential to significantly influence the evolution path of current wireless technologies. The integration of low-power radio, sensor (MEMS), and chip (CMOS) technologies into wireless sensor node devices today enable the widespread use of wireless sensor networks for a number of diverse applications.

Current wireless technologies, such as cellular networks [4], broadband wireless access technologies (WiMax [5]), and wireless local area networks (WLAN [6]) rely on fixed infrastructure. Encouraged by the enormous success of today's pervasive wireless technologies, the research community has focused on exploring ways to extend the bounds of the current communication infrastructure and services, in order to provide less costly, more flexible, reliable and less infrastructure-dependent communication systems. Achieving reliable communication without infrastructure support is the basic principle in the design of mobile ad hoc networks (MANETs) [7].

MANETs are self-configuring networks of mobile hosts/routers, connected by wireless links. These networks are characterized by the highly dynamic changes in network topology (the mobile routers can leave the network area, for example), and by unreliable communication between the hosts, caused by the unpredictable nature of wireless links, which brings many challenges in the design of communication protocols that efficiently overcome these problems. These multi-hop mobile ad hoc networks have been used by the military for a long time, and they became a popular research topic in the mid to late 1990s, when laptops and the IEEE 802.11 standard [8] became widespread.

Along with the appearance of the first MANETs, wireless sensor networks (WSNs) [9] emerged as a special kind of infrastructure-less wireless network with their own unique set of features. Wireless sensor networks consist of smart computing devices — wireless nodes,

1

envisioned as small, robust, and cheap devices that can be deployed in a wide variety of applications and environmental conditions. Equipped with different types of sensors, WSNs achieve tight integration with the physical world. Similar to the nodes in MANETs, sensor nodes act both as hosts as well as routers, operating in a self-organizing and adaptive manner. Usually, sensor nodes do not have the capability to move, but rather they are deployed in an ad hoc manner in an area of interest and left unattended to collect data for long periods of time.

WSNs may contain various types of sensor nodes, in terms of their sensing and processing capabilities. In this book, we investigate various management policies developed with the respect to different sensor types in order to efficiently utilize the resources of a wireless sensor network used for a particular application. Considering the energy constraints of sensor nodes, we first analyze a topology control policy that enables establishing an energy balanced clustered heterogeneous sensor network. Then, we analyze the sensor nodes' role assignment problem in clustered networks, in order to meet application-specific Quality of Service (QoS). Furthermore, we examine various resource management problems in visual sensor networks, where camera-nodes are used as a special type of sensor node, considering the differences between these sensors and those commonly used in "traditional" wireless sensor networks.

1.1   Core Features of Wireless Sensor Networks

The design of wireless sensor networks is determined by the sensor nodes' characteristics and by application-specific requirements. Oftentimes, the sensor network has to satisfy several, sometimes competing constraints, suggesting the need for compromise solutions that provide balance between all of the imposed constraints. The list of design challenges is long; here we indicate some of the most important:

Energy limitations   In the absence of promising energy-scavenging technologies that would provide constant energy supplies for the sensor nodes, batteries are the most commonly used sources of energy. Energy is thus a scarce resource, and it presents a basic limiting factor for the node's lifetime. Thus, intelligent policies for the efficient utilization of the energy resources are needed.

Communication in sensor networks is by far the most expensive operation in terms of energy [10], [11]. As an illustration, it is worth mentioning that the energy required for

2

transmission of only one bit is sufficient for the execution of about a thousand arithmetical operations [12]. In wireless networks, the received signal power varies as a function of distance. This variation is caused by path loss and shadowing. The energy spent for transmission of data packets, in the case of variable transmission power, rises as a function of d^k, where d is the transmission distance and k is the path loss exponent [4]. The propagation of electromagnetic waves (signals) through the medium can be disturbed by various environmental factors, such as presence of obstructing objects or surface roughness, for example, which causes signal absorbtion, reflection, scattering and diffraction [13]. These factors further attenuate the signal power at the receiver, influencing the reception of data packets and thereby increasing the overall energy consumption of the network.

Local processing   Data collected by the sensor nodes that lie in proximity to each other may contain a high level of spatial and temporal redundancy [14]. Local data processing (through data aggregation or data fusion) reduces the amount of data that have to be transmitted back to the data sink, thereby providing the application with high-level data representations that qualitatively satisfy the application's requirements.

Resistance to node failure   Sensor networks are dynamic systems. Changes in the network topology may be caused by node failure due to various factors such as depleted batteries, environmental factors (fire, flood), an intruder's attack, *etc.* The network should be self-adaptable, meaning that the loss of sensor nodes should not affect the overall functionality of the sensor network.

Scalability   In many applications, a sensor network may contain hundreds or even thousands of sensor nodes. The sensor network should be scalable, meaning that the performance of the sensor network should be minimally affected by a change in network size. In many cases, recharging or replacing batteries is not possible, and adding new sensor nodes is the only way to prolong the lifetime of the network. In such cases, the network should easily integrate any new sensor nodes, with minimal degradation of functionality.

Deployment   Sensor nodes can be deployed in various ways, depending on the application and the environmental conditions. They can be deployed randomly over the monitoring field, they can be attached to a specific moving object that is being monitored or they can be arranged deterministically. After deployment, the sensor nodes in most applications remain static. Depending on the deployment strategy, suitable communication protocols should be developed based on the existing network topology in order to support the network's functionality.

Heterogeneity Sensor networks may consist of different types of nodes in terms of their sensing capabilities, computation power, memory size, radio circuitry and energy consumption. The diversity of hardware components can become a gap between these devices, raising new issues in communication and network configuration.

Quality of Service (QoS) Satisfying the application goals by meeting the QoS requirements is one of the basic principles of sensor network design. Quality of service in wireless sensor networks [15] can be defined from two perspectives: application-specific and network. The application-specific QoS refers to QoS parameters specific to the application, such as: the quality of the sensor nodes' measurements, the application-specified network's coverage, the number of active sensors, delay, *etc*. The network's perspective of QoS refers to the problem of how the supporting network can satisfy the application's needs, while efficiently using the network resources such as energy or bandwidth. With the appearance of multimedia applications in wireless sensor networks, as evidenced in visual sensor networks, higher demands on QoS are imposed. In the visual sensor networks the best-effort service cannot provide satisfying level of QoS, meaning that in these type of wireless sensor networks soft QoS needs to be satisfied [16].

1.2   Motivation

Regardless of the specific application, there are several common observations related to the design of any sensor network:

- Energy is a scarce resource in the network. However, minimizing energy consumption does not necessarily prolong the network's lifetime, nor does it ultimately supports the QoS constraints imposed by the specific application.

- The sensor network's design includes finding the best trade-offs between the application's goals and the network's capabilities.

- The number of active sensor nodes should be minimized such that redundancy in sensor readings is minimized, while providing satisfactory quality of data.

- Sensor network design is directed by the type of senor nodes used in the network.

4

Wireless sensor networks provide us with an expanded view of the environment around us. When a large number of spatially close sensors performs data gathering at the same time the redundancy of the sensor readings is high, which without considering the application's minimum requirements can result in expensive transmissions of the gathered data to the sink. However, the network should provide the *relevant* data that is sufficient to satisfy the application-specific requirements, by gathering the information from only a subset of sensor nodes, instead of all available nodes in the network. Along this direction, we explore different methods for the selection of the most suitable set of sensors to satisfy the application QoS requirements in different types of sensor networks.

Sensor nodes are envisioned as multi-functional devices. For example, a sensor node can either sense the environment, coordinate a group of other nodes and process their data, act as a data router, or perform a mix of these operations. In the case of clustered sensor networks, the nodes may have predetermined roles, or they may have assigned roles that change over time, by following the application requirements or energy conservation principle. We investigate how the particular roles in clustered sensor networks can be supported for longer periods by exploring different ways to build clustered network architectures. Also, we explore cluster head election techniques in hierarchically organized sensor networks that must satisfy certain coverage-preserving requirements.

Despite the many challenges in sensor network design, the interest for new applications of these networks is tremendous. We believe that the real potential of wireless sensor networks lies in their integration with other technologies and research fields. This motivates our work on visual sensor networks as a new kind of sensor network that provides visual information of the monitored region.

Therefore, this book is directed toward designing application-aware sensor network architectures and sensor management policies that are needed to support the reduction of redundant data as well as node heterogeneity in order to achieve application-determined quality. In particular, we follow this philosophy through the design and optimization of two specific types of wireless sensor networks: hierarchical (cluster based) sensor networks and visual sensor networks.

1.2.1 Sensor Management for Hierarchical Networks

In the first part of this book our attention is directed toward exploring efficient application-aware resource management policies for hierarchically organized wireless sensor networks. Clustering is a well known approach for energy-efficient and scalable network organization [17–21]. In contrast to cellular networks, where each base station is powered by an essentially limitless source of energy, the cluster heads in wireless sensor networks have a finite amount of energy available. Since the loss of the cluster head nodes usually translates into the loss of data from all the cluster members, we begin by exploring the problem of energy consumption balancing among cluster head nodes in homogeneous and heterogeneous wireless sensor networks.

The multi-modal abilities of sensor nodes enables them to act as data sources, data routers or aggregators of received data. Multi-hop data routing through the network reduces the overall energy consumption of the sensor network, but at the same time quickly exhausts the energy of the sensor nodes that frequently serve as data routers. Our solution to this problem proposes the use of a clustered network architecture with clusters of *unequal sizes* in order to better balance the energy consumption of the sensor nodes. This approach follows the logic that if a sensor node has limited remaining energy, once it becomes a cluster head node, it should support clusters of smaller size than those sensor nodes that have more energy available. In the case of heterogeneous networks, our solution to the problem of unbalanced energy consumption is based on a deterministic deployment of the cluster head sensor nodes.

Furthermore, we analyze how the application-specific QoS requirements can be addressed in a cluster-based wireless sensor network, specifically by looking into the problem of providing complete coverage of the network. We notice that although cluster-based network organization reduces the overall energy consumption in the network, it does not guarantee satisfaction of application coverage requirements for long periods of time. Our approach suggests that both energy constraints and coverage redundancy should be considered in order to find a way to satisfy the application's coverage requirements in clustered sensor networks for longer periods of time.

1.2.2 Sensor Management for Visual Sensor Networks

Through our research on hierarchical sensor networks, we gain valuable knowledge about the importance of application-aware management of sensor networks. We apply this idea to visual sensor networks, as described in the second part of this book.

Visual sensor networks inherit characteristics from both wireless sensor networks and more general ad hoc networks. We first focus on the differences between "traditional" and visual sensor networks, considering the research directions already established in the area of wireless sensor networks. Due to the unique sensing of image sensors, the increased needs for the network's resources and the more strict QoS requirements, not all protocols developed

6

for traditional sensor networks can be used directly in visual sensor networks.

Visual sensor networks provide users with large amounts of information, which makes them extremely resource demanding. The right sensor management policies, in terms of sensor selection and scheduling, become essential in order to provide persistent monitoring. A camera's sensing differs from the sensing of other types of sensors, since it provides *directional* sensing, which enables the camera to capture information from distant parts of the monitored area. The energy consumption is important, but not the only constraint for visual sensor networks. In many applications of visual sensor networks, the goal is to fully cover the entire monitored 3D space with the cameras. Considering the unique characteristics of the camera-nodes, the choice of the right set of cameras for performing the sensing task broadly influences the quality of the data received and the lifetime of the sensor network.

We begin by analyzing how existing routing protocols developed for "traditional" sensor networks behave when applied in visual sensor networks. Then, we explore the influence of different camera-node selection methods on the network's lifetime and the quality of the reconstructed images. We continue the work on resource management policies by looking into the problem of scheduling active camera nodes. Finally, we show how the visual information provided by the cameras can be used in order to improve the precision of an object's position determined by a wireless sensor network based localization system.

1.3   Book Contributions

This book provides analysis of several methods for sensor network organization and sensor management in different types of sensor networks. The specific discussions are:

- We present the Unequal Clustering Size approach that achieves better energy balanced hierarchically organized sensor networks compared with clustering approaches that utilize equal size clusters.

- Based on a family of application-aware cost metrics, we discuss a heuristic for the selection of cluster head nodes, active nodes and routers, as well as a clustering protocol for a hierarchical sensor network, thereby supporting the coverage requirements of the sensor network.

- In visual sensor networks, we first explore the behavior of a coverage-preserving routing protocol that was initially designed for traditional sensor networks, when it is used for data routing in a network of wireless camera-nodes. Then, we provide directions for the design of QoS-aware routing protocols in this kind of network.

- We provide application-aware methods for the selection of camera-nodes in visual sensor networks, with the goal of maximizing the 3D coverage of the monitored area over time. We show the advantage of using a QoS-aware approach for camera selection over other standard selection approaches.

- We analyze the energy-efficient camera scheduling problem in visual sensor networks, where camera-nodes grouped into a number of coverage sets are used to monitor the space of interest.

- Finally, we describe how the camera's image sensing capability can be used for improving a localization service in sensor networks. We describe the localization system implemented in a real testbed consisting of a network of wireless sensor nodes and a camera.

1.4 Book Structure

In Chapter 2 of this book we provide an overview of wireless sensor networks, focusing on topics that are most relevant for the work presented in the first part of this book. We explain the advantages of the unequal clustering approach in homogeneous and heterogeneous networks in Chapter 3. The cluster head selection methods and the clustering protocol for the preservation of the network's coverage are presented and analyzed in Chapter 4. We move out attention to visual sensor networks in Chapter 5, where we first provide an overview of this type of sensor networks. In Chapter 6, we analyze the problem of application-specific routing in visual sensor networks. Our work with visual sensor networks continues in Chapter 7, where we analyze and compare methods for the selection of active cameras. In Chapter 8, we present approaches for the energy-efficient scheduling of camera-nodes. In Chapter 9 we describe a prototype of a positioning system that fuses the location information provided by a wireless sensor network and image information from a camera to find the precise coordinates of an object. Finally, in Chapter 10 we conclude this book and provide directions for future work on clustered sensor networks and visual sensor networks.

Chapter 2

An Overview of Wireless Sensor Networks

In this Chapter, we provide an overview of the most important characteristics, design challenges and metrics for the evaluation of the performance of wireless sensor networks. Our overview begins with general information about the sensor node's hardware and network stack, followed by an overview of applications and related work for wireless sensor networks.

2.1 General Sensor Node Architecture

Over the past few years, a variety of hardware solutions have been proposed for sensor nodes. The ultimate goal is to produce sensor nodes that are small in size, cheap and that last for a very long time, thanks to low-power operations and the low duty-cycle. Today, with respect to the characteristics of wireless sensor networks mentioned in Section 1.1, sensor nodes are still in the early development phase, and still they mainly present prototypes of ongoing research. An extensive overview of the currently available sensor node prototypes is provided in [22].

A sensor node contains several functional components, as shown in Figure 2.1. The microprocessor performs the data processing in order to reduce the amount of data that needs to be transmitted over the wireless medium. Also, it controls the peripherals, such as radio and attached sensor circuitry. When not used, the microprocessor enters low-power modes, thereby significantly decreasing the energy consumption. The radio interface comprises the radio transceiver with power control. Increased transmission power results in smaller probability of dropped packets at the receiver, but at the same time it increases

9

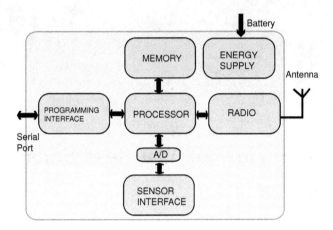

Figure 2.1: General architecture of a wireless sensor node.

the interference with other nodes in the transmission range. Thus, intelligent policies for choosing adequate power levels need to be considered. Different types of sensors can be attached to the node through the sensor interface. Since many sensors have analog output, an additional A/D circuit may be needed to bridge the gap between the sensor and the node.

2.2 Protocol Stack

The general protocol stack of a wireless sensor node consists of several layers, as illustrated in Figure 2.2. The physical layer is responsible for sending and receiving of bits over the wireless channel. It performs several tasks, such as: frequency selection, carrier frequency generation, signal detection, and modulation [23].

The link layer is responsible for applying error correction. The medium access control (MAC) layer controls the access of a sensor node to the shared radio channel. The MAC layer has information about one-hop links, such as the channel condition and packet loss rates. This layer controls different operation modes [24] (e.g. transmit/receive, idle, sleep) of a node. Therefore, the MAC layer has a large impact on the energy efficiency of the sensor nodes [25–27]. The traditional QoS requirements of wireless MAC protocols, such as those related to channel bandwidth utilization, delay, fairness or throughput, may not be the major concerns in very low data rate wireless sensor networks. However, these goals are of concern for the new generations of real-time multimedia sensor networks.

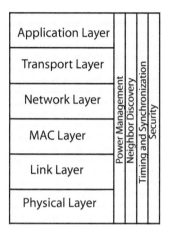

Figure 2.2: The protocol stack and cross-layer services.

The network layer is responsible for discovering routes between the sensor nodes in multihop wireless sensor networks. Routing should be energy-efficient and stable, and it should support various QoS (end-to-end) requirements. The network layer should have knowledge of the end-to-end characteristics of the route. Routing in wireless sensor networks should support the data-centric nature of sensor networks, which requires attribute-based instead of ID-based addressing of sensor nodes [28, 29].

The transport layer is concerned with the congestion control and reliable delivery of packets. Traditional transport protocols, such as TCP, are not suitable for use in sensor networks. For example, TCP assumes that the primary cause of packet loss is congestion that occurs in the network; however, packet loss in sensor networks occurs mostly due to interference or low power transmission.

The application layer is the only layer on the network stack that directly interacts with the user. It implements the application requirements and performs data acquisition and analysis.

The application layer usually does not have information about the network state, nor does the MAC layer have information about the end-to-end route, since the design of each layer is done separately. However, the operations of one layer strongly affect the functionality of all the other layers, suggesting that the independent design of every network layer should be replaced by a cross-layer design approach. Several papers [23, 30], emphasize the importance of cross-layer services that are shared among all the layers of the network stack, as illustrated in Figure 2.2. A cross-layer design approach, which considers the joint performance of all layers, should be used in order to optimize the performances of the sensor network.

2.3 Applications of Wireless Sensor Networks

The number of wireless sensor network applications increases rapidly. Some of the applications of wireless sensor networks are:

- Environmental monitoring - Wireless sensor network can be used for monitoring a broad spectrum of environmental variables. One of the first projects that considered the deployment of wireless sensor networks for habitat monitoring was done by UC Berkeley [31], where sensor nodes were placed on Great Duck Island in order to track the nest occupation of bird colonies, and to collect data about the environmental conditions such as temperature, barometric pressure or humidity.

- Medical Monitoring - Wireless sensor networks in medical applications are used to provide help in emergency situations, when medical equipment is out of reach or when on-time medical response is essential. Also, in the rehabilitation process for patients, medical monitoring can be provided by wireless sensor nodes that continuously measure vital statistics such as heart rate, EKG or blood oxygen level [32].

- Industrial Monitoring and Control - Since wireless sensor networks eliminate the need for infrastructure deployment and enable flexible network configurations, they can be easily adopted for various industrial monitoring applications, such as pipeline or power line monitoring. However, in these applications the sensor nodes must be able to withstand harsh environments, meaning that the network must be failure resistant and self-configurable in order to avoid single points of failure.

- Building Automation - This set of applications include sensor networks deployed in public and commercial buildings. For example, sensor networks deployed in a hotel can be used for room control, control of HVAC systems, or building structure monitoring.

- Military Applications - Wireless ad hoc network technology has been used for military purposes for a long time. Wireless sensors can be deployed easily (by throwing them from an aircraft, for example), to collect various data from a battlefield, and to collect data about the enemy (for example, to track the enemy through some region).

2.4 Related Work

The research related to efficient resource utilization strategies in wireless sensor networks covers various aspects, including those related to the routing, network topology and sensor management policies. The work related to these aspects are presented in the following Section.

2.4.1 Energy Consumption

In most applications, self-configuring wireless sensor networks are envisioned to last for months or even years. The replacement of the batteries for a large number of sensor nodes is often not an option, so in order to last longer, sensor networks must have a low-power profile, achieved through the coherent design of both hardware and the networking stack, providing a trade-off between energy consumption, functional fidelity and lifetime of the sensor network. There are several factors that affect the energy consumption of the sensor node.

The radio circuit often consumes the highest amount of energy, which depends on the hardware as well as the type of modulation and transmission power. The transmission power depends on the transmission distance, and on previous radio devices the radio transceiver consumed significantly larger amounts of energy for transmission than for reception. However, the power consumption of the radio circuitry in the receive mode for newer generations of sensor node platforms (Telos [33], for example) is comparable, if not even slightly higher than the power consumption in the transmit mode. Also, the transitions from one transceiver mode to the other are followed by noneligible energy dissipation and introduce latency overhead for the application [34].

The choice of modulation scheme greatly affects the energy consumption as well as the latency in the sensor node's response. Earlier platforms for sensor nodes (e.g., Mica, Mica2, or Rene [35]) used narrowband radios, that use simple modulation schemes (OOK, ASK, FSK) and provide fast start-up, but they do not use signal spreading, making the radio signal sensitive to noise. The newer platforms (e.g., Telos [33]) use wideband radios based on more complex modulation techniques (OQPSK), and they use direct sequence spread spectrum (DSSS) to increase the channel reliability and noise tolerance.

Today, there are a wide variety of processors available, each of which offer different processing capabilities for different power consumption profiles, so the general rule is to choose the processor to best suite the application. The processor/microcontroller can switch between different operational modes (active, sleep, idle), which are usually characterized by different power consumption.

The power consumption of the sensors attached to the wireless nodes strongly depends on the type of sensor. Some sensors, such as temperature, or seismic sensors, have negligible power consumption. Other sensors, such as image sensors, are characterized by very high power consumption. In the latter case, a significant part of the energy is spent for expensive analog-to-digital conversions (ADC) [36].

2.4.2 Routing

The first routing protocols developed for wireless ad hoc networks were strongly influenced by the routing protocols already developed for the Internet, where the cost for routing is proportional to the number of hops to reach the final destination (shortest hop algorithm). However, these protocols were found not to be suitable for ad hoc networks for a number of reasons. First, the transmission of data through Ethernet is characterized by extremely low probabilities of bit errors. Also, wired networks contain a backbone network formed by a number of very powerful routers, with virtually unlimited energy supply and memory. On the other hand, ad hoc networks essentially do not rely on any existing infrastructure. The lifetimes of the wireless nodes strongly depend on their battery supply. The wireless channel is an extremely unreliable medium, with a very high probability of error. These facts motivated new research related to improved routing in mobile ad hoc networks and wireless sensor networks over the last decade.

2.4.3 Energy Aware Routing

Energy-aware routing considers the energy constraints of the wireless nodes in the process of finding the best path from a source to a destination. Singh et al. [37] proposed several routing metrics based on the node's battery power consumption, which significantly reduces the routing cost of the packets compared to shortest path routing. The lifetime of the nodes can be prolonged by selecting paths that do not use nodes with low remaining energy. According to this, the path selection for packet j minimizes the total routing cost c_j for sending packet j from node n_1 to node n_k:

$$c_j = \sum_{i=1}^{k-1} f_i(x_i) \tag{2.1}$$

where $f_i(x_i)$ is the cost of node i along the routing path, represented by the total energy x_i expended by this node so far.

Chang et al. [38] analyzed the problem of routing path selection between a source and a sink, so that the time until the first node exhausts its battery is maximized. They noticed that routes with the total minimum energy expenditure do not necessarily prolong the nodes' lifetime, since some of the nodes can be excessively burdened with a high relaying load. They proposed two algorithms for solving this problem. The first algorithm (called flow redirection algorithm) is based on the fact that if the minimum lifetime of a node along two paths is different, then the lifetime of a node along the path with the shorter lifetime can be increased by redirecting a part of the traffic from this path to other paths. The second algorithm (called the flow augmentation algorithm) uses the Bellman-Ford algorithm and balances the load among the nodes in proportion to their remaining energy. The link costs c_{ij} between nodes i and j are found as:

$$c_{ij} = e_{ij}^{x_1} \underline{E_i}^{-x_2} E_i^{x_3} \tag{2.2}$$

where e_{ij} represents the transmission energy from node i to node j, E_i represents node i's initial energy and $\underline{E_i}$ is the remaining energy of node i. The optimal values (x_1, x_2, x_3) are found through simulations. This algorithm outperforms the flow redirection algorithm, since it considers the current energy status of the nodes.

Toh et al. [39] proposed the min-max battery cost routing (MMBCR) and conditional max-min battery capacity routing (CMMBCR) algorithms for the selection of source-to-destination paths. The MMBCR algorithm selects a path from the source to the destination along which the minimum of the residual energies of the sensors is maximized. The CMM-BCR finds the minimum energy paths from the source to the destination in which no node has residual energy below a threshold. If such a path cannot be found, then the MMBCR algorithm is used.

Li et al. [40] proposed the *max-min* zP_{min} algorithm for route selection. This algorithm selects the path that uses at most $z \cdot P_{min}$ energy, where z is a parameter of the algorithm and P_{min} is the energy required by the minimum-energy path. The selected path maximizes the minimum residual energy fraction (energy remaining after route/initial energy) of the nodes on the route. Possible values for the residual energy fraction of a node i can be obtained by computing $(E_c(i) - v(i, j))/E_r(i)$, where $E_c(i)$ is the current energy at node i just before the route, $v(i, j)$ is the cost of the edge (i, j) and $E_r(i)$ is node's i remaining energy. This computation is done for all vertices j adjacent to i.

15

2.4.4 Data Centric Routing Protocols

In a sensor network, the nodes are distinguished according to the data collected, which eliminates the need for global node identification. Therefore, data retrieval from the sensor network is commonly based on data-centric rather than address-centric queries.

SPIN [41] was the first routing protocol that considered this fact. The SPIN-1 protocol is designed for effective data dissemination following a 3-way handshake procedure (ADV-REQ-DATA) between adjacent nodes, initiated by the data source nodes. Sensor nodes use high-level names for their data, called meta-data, for negotiation with other nodes before the data transmission, thereby avoiding the transmission of redundant data. In the SPIN-2 protocol sensor nodes have access to their current energy levels. Therefore, as a node approaches a low-energy threshold, it reduces its participation in the protocol.

Directed diffusion [29] is a destination-initiated data centric routing protocol. The nodes name their data by one or more attributes. Based on these attributes, the destination (sink) floods the network with *interests* (queries). Upon reception of an interest from a neighbor, a sensor node sets up a *gradient* (consisting of event rate and direction toward the destination) to send data to the neighbor. Gradient is stored in the node's local cache together with the interest's type and duration. If the node receives the same interest from several neighbors, multiple paths can be set up from the data source to the sink. The sink node may reinforce high quality paths upon receiving low rate data from the source nodes. Also, directed diffusion enables intermediate nodes to aggregate data, thereby improving the energy efficiency of the network.

2.4.5 QoS-aware Routing Protocols

Routing in power-constrained sensor networks should consider the application's requirements (for example, demands for full coverage, delay tolerance, reliability). Multi-hop transmission is often considered to be the most efficient way to route data through a network. However, multi-hop routing results in increased delay for the data packets, due to queuing and processing at the intermediate nodes. Since end-to-end delay usually increases with the number of hops, QoS-aware routing protocols are often concerned with the energy-latency trade-off, providing expected delay guarantees through balancing the number of hops, the delay requirements and the energy consumption.

The time-varying nature of the wireless channel makes it difficult for the network to achieve hard QoS requirements, but soft QoS can be provided [42]. One of the most successful routing protocols designed to achieve soft QoS is SPEED [43]. Since the end-to-end delay in a multi-hop network depends on distance a packet travels, SPEED routes packets according to the packet's *maximum delivery speed*, which presents the rate at which the packet travels along a straight line to the destination. The routing algorithm determines the transmission delay of the packet considering its end-to-end distance and its delivery speed. When the maximum delivery speed cannot be achieved due to network congestion, SPEED uses a *back-pressure rerouting* scheme, which avoids routing packets over the congested links while achieving the desired delivery speed.

Coverage is another important QoS metric in wireless sensor networks. DAPR [44] is a routing protocol integrated with a sensor activation protocol, designed for applications that require persistent full coverage of the monitored area over time. DAPR considers coverage redundancy as well as the nodes' remaining energy in route selection. This approach favors routing the data through areas that are more densely populated with sensor nodes, thereby alleviating the nodes that are not redundantly covered by their neighbors from the additional routing load. The contribution of each sensor node to the coverage task is expressed by an application-specific cost metric. The final cost of each node is the cost of the route through which data is sent back to the sink. Decisions about the activation of each sensor node are brought based on its final cost as well as by considering whether the area under its sensing range is already covered by its neighboring nodes. By this, only a subset of sensor nodes required to maximally cover the monitored area is activated in each communication round, thereby reducing the coverage redundancy by the sensor nodes over the monitored area.

2.4.6 Clustering Algorithms

With an increase in the number of nodes in the sensor network, issues such as load balancing, scalability, and energy efficiency become particularly important in determining network lifetime. Clustering is one of the basic approaches for providing energy efficient, robust and highly scalable distributed sensor networks. In a hierarchically organized cluster-based sensor network spatially close nodes are grouped into a cluster centered around a cluster head node, which manages the rest of the nodes in the cluster. Cluster head nodes are responsible for various tasks, including gathering data from the sensor nodes within the cluster, data processing and aggregation/fusion of the data, and transmission of the collected data to other cluster head nodes or to the main processing center (i.e. the sink or the base station).

Wireless sensor networks organized into clusters can be broadly classified as homogeneous and heterogeneous networks, depending on the type and the functionality of the sensor nodes in the network. All sensor nodes in a *homogeneous* sensor network have the same hardware and equal processing capabilities. Sensor nodes usually rotate the cluster head roles among themselves, which assures more uniform energy spending among the nodes in the network. In *heterogeneous* cluster-based sensor networks the cluster head roles can be preassigned to a specific group of high-power nodes (the nodes with enhanced processing capabilities, more memory and larger energy supplies than the rest of the low-power nodes). To filter out redundant data, the cluster head nodes can aggregate data from the sensors before sending the data back to the sink. Apart from a reduction in energy consumption, cluster-based organization of the sensor network enables frequency reuse, thereby limiting interference in the communication of spatially close clusters.

2.4.7 Homogeneous Cluster-based Sensor Networks

LEACH [17] was among the first proposed clustering-based protocols that utilized randomized rotation of cluster heads to evenly distribute the energy consumption among the sensor nodes in the network. LEACH incorporates data aggregation into the routing protocol to reduce the amount of data transmitted to the base station. The cluster heads are chosen probabilistically so that nodes with higher remaining energy are more likely to become cluster heads in the upcoming round. Each cluster head acts as a gateway between the cluster members and the base station. The probabilistic approach for clustering in LEACH has a small implementation cost, which makes it attractive for realistic implementations. At the same time, this approach makes the system less predictable due to the random number of clusters formed in each communication round. An extension to LEACH, called LEACH-C, ameliorates this problem. LEACH-C uses simulating annealing to find the cluster heads such that the average transmission power between the cluster head and its cluster members is minimized. However, this requires global knowledge of sensor node positions and current energy.

Homogeneous cluster-based sensor networks were also investigated in [20], where the authors found the optimal clustering parameters such as the probability of becoming a cluster head and the cluster radius by minimizing the communication cost of the network. Based on this the authors proposed a distributed clustering algorithm to organize the network into single and multi-level clusters.

Younis et al. [18] proposed a distributed clustering algorithm called HEED that is based on an iterative clustering process that terminates within a constant number of iterations. HEED produces well distributed clusters, it minimizes the control overhead and the cluster-

18

ing process does not depend on the network topology or network size. Cluster head selection is based on the nodes' residual energy and intra-cluster communication cost. The communication cost is a function of the cluster properties (such as cluster size), and it depends on whether the nodes can use the minimum required power or they all use the same power to reach the cluster head. HEED uses the nodes' residual energies to probabilistically select an initial set of cluster heads. In each iteration, every node that did not hear the announcement message from a potential cluster head probabilistically elects itself as a tentative cluster head. In every iteration the probability of becoming a cluster head is doubled for each sensor node. The sensor node elects itself as a new cluster head when its cluster head probability reaches one. More details about this protocol are provided in Section 4.6.1.

In [21] the authors presented the ACE (Algorithm for Cluster Establishment) clustering algorithm, which divides the sensor network into uniformly dispersed clusters. ACE achieves uniform clusters by reducing the overlap among the clusters established in the initial phase. Those nodes that have the largest number of either "uncovered" neighbors or neighbors in non-overlapping cluster areas are recruited as favorable new cluster head nodes.

The problem of scheduling nodes to enter the sleep mode in cluster-based sensor networks was studied in [45]. The authors proposed a linear distance-based sleep scheduling scheme, where the probability that a sensor enters the sleeping state is proportional to its distance from the cluster head. Since such a scheme leads to unequal energy consumption of sensor nodes in the cluster, the same problem is further investigated in [46]. Here the authors present a balanced energy scheduling scheme, which accounts for the total energy spent in communication and sensing, thereby assuring that energy is uniformly dissipated by the nodes.

2.4.8 Heterogeneous Cluster-based Sensor Networks

Mhatre et al. [47] present a comparative study of homogeneous and heterogeneous clustered sensor networks where the clusters are organized as either single-hop or multi-hop clusters. They consider the desirable characteristics of sensor networks: low hardware cost and uniform energy consumption. The authors compare both types of networks considering the overall networking cost, thereby providing an energy-hardware trade-off. They found that for the case when the propagation loss index is high ($k > 2$), single-hop communication within a cluster is not an optimum choice. They extend the LEACH protocol to M-LEACH, where the cluster members route data to the cluster head through multi-hop paths, achieving by this additional energy savings among the sensor nodes.

Smaragdakis et al. propose SEP (Stable Election Protocol) [48], which studies the impact of the heterogeneity of nodes, in terms of their energy, in clustered wireless sensor networks. They assume an application that depends on the reliability of the nodes' responses, for which the death of the first node is referred to as the stability period. SEP is based on weighted election probabilities of each node to become cluster head according to the remaining energy in each node, which can prolong the stability period and improve the throughput.

2.4.9   Sensor Management in WSN

In many application scenarios the sensor nodes are deployed densely over the monitored field. The data collected from these nodes usually contain redundant information. Although the redundancy in sensor readings increases the reliability of the collected information, at the same time the transmission of this data presents huge overhead for the network.

Oftentimes data gathered from only a subset of sensor nodes instead of all sensor nodes can be sufficient for the application. The intelligent scheduling of the sensor nodes manages available resources (e.g., energy and bandwidth), while meeting certain QoS requirements imposed by the application (such as demand to maximize coverage, minimize delay or to achieve application-specific data resolution/fidelity). Therefore, one of the problems that has intrigued the research community over the last few years is the problem of how to utilize the redundancy in the sensors' deployment in order to provide benefits to the application. This requires finding energy-efficient collaborative strategies that will govern sensor nodes to jointly perform the sensing task.

Efficient sensor scheduling protocols determine whether a sensor node should be active or in sleep mode, how long the sensor node should stay in each state, and under what conditions the sensor node should change its state. There are many factors that influence the design of efficient sensor scheduling protocols, such as:

- sensing/communication range — these ranges can broadly influence the performance of the network, mostly affecting connectivity (as explained in [49]), sensing redundancy and energy consumption.

- coverage degree — some applications require more redundancy in the data extracted from the sensor network [50].

- deployment — in general, management protocols for sensor scheduling and selection may be different in cases when the nodes are deployed in a deterministic manner.

- nodes' functionality — as stated previously, sensor nodes can support multiple functions, which raises the problem of assigning different roles to the sensor nodes in the an optimal way for the particular application.

For example, in [51] the authors look into the problem of assigning different roles (sensing, relaying, aggregating) from the *feasible role assignment set* (FRA) to the nodes in a sensor network, which will allow sensing in a non-redundant manner. The authors provide an upper bound of the network lifetime for the optimal collaboration strategy of the nodes. However, their role assignment technique is computationally cumbersome, which justifies the use of other heuristic solutions for sensor role assignments.

One of the fundamental metrics for the qualification of sensor network performance is coverage. The coverage metric tells us how well a physical space is monitored by the sensor nodes [52]. One of the first algorithms for coverage preservation was proposed in [53], where each node determines if it should be turned on or off based on whether its sensing area is already covered by the sensing areas of its neighboring nodes. The node covers the "sector" (central angle) of the sensing range of its neighboring node. In order to prevent situations when two neighboring nodes simultaneously decide to turn off, which can result in the appearance of blind spots, the nodes evaluate their status after a random time, after which they broadcast their decision to their neighboring nodes.

In a densely populated networks the application may require coverage with different degrees. In [49] the authors present the Coverage Configuration Protocol (CCP) that deals with this problem. The activation decision is brought at every sensor node by considering the coverage of the intersection points of its sensing range with the sensing ranges of the rest of the nodes. In order to inform its neighbors of its current position and status, nodes periodically broadcast HELLO messages. Nodes switch between three possible states: ACTIVE, SLEEP and LISTEN. In the ACTIVE state nodes sense the environment and communicate with other nodes. They periodically enter the LISTEN state and collect HELLO messages from other nodes to determine their new state. However, this algorithm does not guarantee connectivity among the sensor nodes when the node's communication range is larger than twice the sensing range. This was fixed by integrating CCP with SPAN [54]. SPAN is a decentralized protocol for topology control that turns off unnecessary nodes while maintaining a communication backbone of active nodes. The combined algorithms can provide the k-coverage of CCP and the 1-connectivity of SPAN.

PEAS [55] is another protocol designed to provide coverage with the goal of keeping only a small number of nodes in the active state, without the additional complexity of maintaining per-neighbor states or determining the duration of active states of working nodes. The nodes wake up after an exponential sleeping period, and they send PROBE messages within a probing range. If the node hears a REPLY from any active node, it goes back to the sleeping mode; otherwise, it activates. The performance of the algorithm is determined by two parameters: the probing range and the wake-up rate. In applications that require robustness, the probing range should be small to achieve a high density of active nodes. To keep the protocol's overhead (which depends on the nodes' wake-ups), constant the authors in [55] propose an *adaptive sleeping* mechanism, which adjusts the wake-up periods of sleeping nodes according to an aggregated probing rate that each node receives from its neighbors. The nodes include information about the probing rate in their REPLY messages, which other nodes use to adjust their sleeping periods.

The problem of achieving full coverage in wireless sensor networks was explored in [56]. The proposed algorithm (OGDC) tries to minimize the number of active nodes by reducing the overlapped area between the active sensors. To ensure that different nodes are active in each round, the starting node broadcasts a power-on message in a random direction along which working nodes are found. A node decides to turn off if it covers an intersection point between two active sensors and if it minimizes the overlapped area with active sensors. However, nodes do not consider the energy levels of their neighbors, so they can send the power-on messages in the direction of nodes with low remaining energy.

Chapter 3

Energy Balanced Clustered Sensor Network Architectures

In most applications the sensor network must operate unattended for a long period of time. In order for the network to maintain the same level of functionality over this period, the energy consumption of the sensor nodes has to be controlled. In this Chapter we introduce and analyze a novel approach for organizing wireless sensor network into the clusters of unequal sizes. The *unequal clustering* approach can prolong the lifetime of both heterogeneous and homogeneous cluster-based sensor networks by balancing the energy consumption among the cluster head nodes.

3.1 Introduction

The energy consumption of a sensor node, and therefore its lifetime, is determined by the node's role in the network as well as by its location within the network. For applications where all sensors are equally important non-uniform energy consumption of sensor nodes degrades the overall performance of the network over time, leading to the appearance of "hot spot" areas where sensor nodes die much earlier than the nodes in the rest of the network. Besides loosing data from this part of the network, hot spot areas may further cause network partitioning, inducing the loss of data from the rest of the network. In order to preserve the desired functionality of the sensor network for longer periods of time, rather than trying only to minimize the energy consumption of the sensor nodes, the sensor network has to balance energy consumption among the nodes as well.

Sensor nodes can be organized hierarchically, by grouping them into clusters. If the network is homogeneous, sensor nodes can be simply randomly deployed over the area of interest. In the case of heterogeneous networks, deterministic deployment of the sensor nodes enables better control of the network's topology obtained by placing the nodes and/or super-nodes at exact predetermined positions. Since the super-nodes serve as the cluster-head nodes, predetermined placement of these nodes allows us to control the size of their clusters.

In both heterogeneous and homogeneous cluster-based sensor networks, the cluster head roles are assigned to the most suitable nodes (those with the most remaining energy, highest processing speed, etc.). However, this is not sufficient to prevent the appearance of hot-spot areas in the network. Cluster head nodes usually form the network backbone and use multi-hop routing to transfer data to the sink. In such a scenario, the cluster head nodes close to the sink are the nodes in the hot-spot area, since they are used more frequently to route data from the rest of the network to the sink. Therefore, by controlling the amount of data that every cluster head node processes and transmits, we can prevent the premature loss of the most critical cluster head nodes—those that are close to the sink.

In this part of the book, we explore the problem of unbalanced energy consumption in clustered wireless sensor networks, with special attention paid to the energy consumption of the cluster head nodes in deterministically deployed heterogeneous sensor networks. As one way to overcome this problem, we introduce a novel clustering technique, by which the cluster sizes are determined such that more balanced energy consumption is achieved among the cluster head nodes [57]. In contrast to existing clustering methods [18], [21], which provide clusters of similar sizes across the network, our novel clustering technique produces clusters of unequal sizes within the network. Furthermore, we show that the proposed clustering approach can be efficiently extended to homogeneous sensor networks as well. Following this approach, we explore the benefits of using the "unequal cluster size" method in homogeneous sensor networks with static and dynamic clusters.

3.2   Unequal Clustering Approach

In cluster-based wireless sensor networks, cluster head nodes spend energy on inter-cluster and intra-cluster communication. The energy spent by a cluster head node in intra-cluster communication (within its cluster) changes proportionally to the number of nodes in the cluster. The energy required for inter-cluster communication (communication with other cluster heads and with the data sink) by a cluster head node is a function of the expected amount of data that this cluster head routes toward the sink. By placing the cluster head nodes deterministically in the monitored area, we can change the sizes of the clusters (and by this, the number of sensor nodes within the clusters, assuming a uniform deployment of sensor nodes), as well as the expected relay load of every cluster head. By this, we can achieve more uniform energy consumption among the cluster head nodes and prevent the premature appearance of "holes"— uncovered parts of the network, that are the result of the loss of cluster head nodes. Therefore, we deal with the problem of unbalanced energy consumption particularly among the cluster head nodes in a heterogeneous network, assuming that these nodes have the highest importance in the network among all sensor nodes, since loss of one of these nodes can cause the loss of data from the entire area under their supervision.

3.3   System Scenario

We consider a sensor network of N nodes randomly deployed over a circular area of radius R_a. In addition to sensor nodes that collect data, a smaller number of more powerful nodes are deployed to serve as cluster head nodes with pre-determined locations. The base station is located in the center of the observed area, and it collects data from the network. The data from all sensors in the cluster are collected at the cluster head, which aggregates the data and forwards the aggregated data toward the base station. The forwarding of aggregated packets is done through multiple hops, where every cluster head chooses to forward its data to the closest cluster head in the direction of the base station.

As stated previously, the positions of the cluster head nodes are determined a priori, with all cluster head nodes arranged symmetrically in concentric circles around the base station. Every cluster is composed of nodes in the Voronoi region around the cluster head. This represents a layered network, as shown in Figure 3.1a for a two layer network, where every layer contains a particular number of clusters. We assume that the inner layer (layer 1) has m_1 clusters and the outer layer (layer 2) has m_2 clusters. Furthermore, in order to simplify the analysis of this model, we approximate the Voronoi regions as pie shaped regions (Figure 3.1b). Due to the symmetrical (circular) organization of cluster head nodes, all clusters in one layer have the same size and shape, but the sizes and shapes of clusters in the two layers are different. We introduce the parameter R_1, which is the radius of the first layer around the base station. By varying the radius R_1, while assuming a constant number of clusters in every layer, the area covered by clusters in each layer can be changed, and therefore the number of nodes contained in a particular cluster is changed.

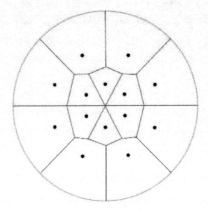

(a) The Voronoi tessellation of a network where cluster heads are arranged circularly around the base station.

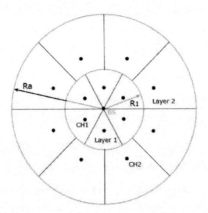

(b) Pie shaped clusters arranged in two layers around the base station. Note that this model, used for analytic simplicity, approximates the Voronoi tessellation of the network.

Figure 3.1: An example of the network topology and its approximation.

Many authors in the literature assume that cluster heads have the ability to perfectly aggregate multiple incoming packets into one outgoing packet. Although this scenario is highly desirable, it is limited to cases when the data are all highly correlated. When this is not the case, or in cases when higher reliability of collected data is desired, the base station can simply demand more than one packet from every cluster head. In such a case, every cluster head will send more than one packet of aggregated data in each round. Therefore, we consider two cases of data aggregation: *perfect aggregation*, when every cluster head compresses all the data received from its cluster into one outgoing packet, and *non-perfect* aggregation, when every cluster head sends more than one packet toward the base station. We do not deal with the particular data aggregation algorithm, but only with the amount of data generated in the aggregation process. We assume that all cluster heads can equally successfully compress the data, where this efficiency is expressed by the aggregation coefficient α.

Time is divided into communication rounds, where one round comprises the time for inter-cluster and intra-cluster communication. The final amount of data forwarded from every cluster head to the base station in one round is $\alpha \cdot N_c$, where N_c is the number of nodes in the cluster and α is in the range $[1/N_c, 1]$. Thus $\alpha = 1/N_c$ represents the case of perfect aggregation, while $\alpha = 1$ represents the case when the cluster head does not perform any aggregation of the packets.

The model for energy dissipation is taken from [17], where, for our multi-hop forwarding model we assume a free space propagation channel model. The energy spent for transmission of a p-bit packet over distance d is:

$$E_{tx} = p \cdot (e_{amf} + e_{fs} \cdot d^n) \tag{3.1}$$

and the energy spent on receiving a p-bit packet is:

$$E_{rx} = p \cdot e_{amf}. \tag{3.2}$$

The parameters e_{amf} and e_{fs} are the parameters of the transmission/reception circuitry, given as $e_{amf} = 50nJ/bit$ and $e_{fs} = 10pJ/bit/m^2$ [17]. We assume the free space propagation model [4], therefore the path-loss coefficient n is set to 2. We assume that the medium is contention free and error free and we do not consider the control messages exchanged between the nodes, assuming that they are very short and do not introduce large overhead.

The position of a cluster head within the cluster boundaries determines the overall energy consumption of nodes that belong to the cluster. To keep the total energy dissipation within the cluster as small as possible, every cluster head should be positioned at the centroid of

27

the cluster. In this case, the distances of cluster heads in layer 1 and layer 2 to the base station are given as [58]:

$$d_{ch1} = \frac{\int_0^{R_1} r \cdot 2 \cdot r \cdot sin(\frac{\beta_1}{2}) \cdot dr}{R_1^2 \cdot \frac{\beta_1}{2}} = \frac{2}{3} \cdot R_1 \cdot \frac{sin(\frac{\beta_1}{2})}{\frac{\beta_1}{2}} \tag{3.3}$$

$$d_{ch2} = \frac{\int_{R_1}^{R_a} r \cdot 2 \cdot r sin(\frac{\beta_2}{2}) \cdot dr}{(R_a^2 - R_1^2) \cdot \frac{\beta_2}{2}} = \frac{2}{3} \cdot \frac{R_a^3 - R_1^3}{R_a^2 - R_1^2} \cdot \frac{sin(\frac{\beta_2}{2})}{\frac{\beta_2}{2}}, \tag{3.4}$$

where β_1 and β_2 are the angles determined by the number of cluster heads in each layer, as $\beta_i = \frac{2\pi}{m_i}$, $i \in [1, 2]$.

In this scenario the network has been divided into clusters during an initial set-up phase, and these clusters remain unchanged during the network lifetime. It is desirable that all cluster heads last as long as possible and die at approximately the same time to avoid network partitioning and loss of sensing coverage. Therefore, we define *network lifetime* as the time when the first cluster head exhausts its energy supply.

The energy consumed by cluster head nodes in layer 1 and layer 2 in one round is described by the following equations:

$$E_{ch1} = p \cdot e_{amf}(N_{cl1} - 1) + p \cdot e_f N_{cl1} + \alpha p \cdot N_{cl2} \frac{m_2}{m_1} e_{amf} +$$
$$+ p \cdot \alpha (N_{cl2} \frac{m_2}{m_1} + N_{cl1})(e_{amf} + e_{fs} d_{ch1}^2) \tag{3.5}$$

$$E_{ch2} = p \cdot e_{amf}(N_{cl2} - 1) + p \cdot e_f N_{cl2} + \alpha p \cdot N_{cl2}(e_{amf} + e_{fs} d_{ch21}^2), \tag{3.6}$$

where d_{ch21} is the distance from a cluster head in layer 2 to a cluster head in layer 1 and d_{ch1} is the distance from a cluster head in layer 1 to the base station. The energy spent for data aggregation is expressed by the parameter $e_f = 5nJ/bit/signal$. N_{cl1} is the number of nodes for clusters in layer 1, and N_{cl2} is the number of nodes for clusters in layer 2, which is proportional to the area covered by the cluster:

$$N_{cl1} = N \frac{R_1^2}{R_a^2 m_1} \tag{3.7}$$

$$N_{cl2} = N \frac{R_a^2 - R_1^2}{R_a^2 m_2}. \tag{3.8}$$

The factor $\frac{m_2}{m_1}$ in equation 3.5 comes from the fact that all packets from the outer layer are equally split on m_1 cluster heads in the inner network layer.

28

3.4   Analysis of the Unequal Clustering Model

We present the evaluation of energy consumption for two hierarchical (clustered) network models. The first model is one commonly used in the literature, where the network is divided into clusters of approximately the same size. We call this model Equal Clustering Size (ECS). For the second model, we use the two-layered network model described previously, where the cluster sizes in each layer are different. We want to find, based on the amount of energy every cluster head spends during one round of communication, how many nodes each cluster should contain so that the total amount of energy spent by all cluster head nodes is equal. We call our approach Unequal Clustering Size (UCS). The variable that directly determines the sizes of clusters in every layer is the radius of the first layer R_1, shown in Figure 3.1b. For ECS, the radius of the first layer is obtained from the fact that the area covered by a cluster in layer 1 is approximately equal to the area of a cluster in layer 2:

$$\frac{R_1^2 \cdot \pi}{m_1} = \frac{(R_a^2 - R_1^2)\pi}{m_2} \tag{3.9}$$

From this, we can obtain the radius of the first layer for the ECS model, R_{eq}:

$$R_{eq} = R_a\sqrt{\frac{m_1}{m_1 + m_2}}. \tag{3.10}$$

In the case of UCS model, there is no closed form solution for the radius of the first network layer.

3.4.1   Cluster Sizes in UCS and ECS Models

Assuming that all cluster head nodes in the UCS model spend the same amount of energy in one communication round, based on equations 3.5 and 3.6 we determine the value of radius R_1 for different numbers of clusters formed in each layer (which is controlled by the parameters m_1, m_2) and for different aggregation efficiency of the cluster heads (controlled by the aggregation coefficient α). For each value of R_1 we calculate the number of nodes that clusters in layer 1 and layer 2 should contain using equations 3.7 and 3.8.

The ratio of the number of nodes for a cluster in layer 1 and a cluster in layer 2 for UCS is shown in Figure 3.2. This result shows that clusters in layer 1 should contain fewer nodes than the clusters in layer 2. The ratio of the number of nodes varies with the number of clusters in each layer, as well as with the aggregation coefficient. The difference in cluster sizes increases as the network less efficiently aggregates the data. We note that this ratio is always less then one, which is the characteristic for ECS. This confirms our intuition, that

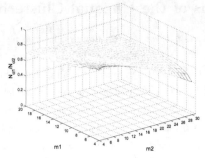

(a) Every cluster head sends 1 aggregated packet.

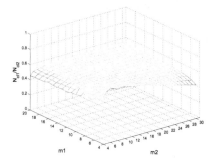

(b) The cluster heads perform aggregation with efficiency $\alpha = 0.1$.

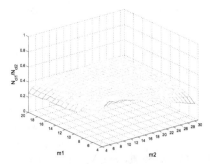

(c) The cluster heads perform aggregation with efficiency $\alpha = 1$.

Figure 3.2: The ratio of the number of nodes in clusters of layer 1 and 2 for the UCS network model.

cluster heads located near the base station and burdened with relaying traffic from the rest of the network, should support fewer cluster members.

When cluster heads compress data more efficiently, meaning that they send fewer packets to the base station, the difference between R_1 obtained for UCS with R_{eq} for ECS gets smaller. This leads to the conclusion that when the aggregation is close to "perfect aggregation," the cluster sizes for UCS should converge to the same size, as in ECS. However, even in the case when cluster heads send only one packet (i.e., perfect aggregation), we find that there should be a difference in cluster sizes in layer 1 and layer 2, as shown in Figure 3.2a. Therefore, the amount of load that burdens every relaying cluster head strongly influences the actual number of nodes that should be supported in the cluster in order to balance energy usage in the network.

3.4.2 Battery Dimensioning for Nodes in the UCS and ECS Network Models

We compare the amount of energy spent by cluster head nodes in both models. Let the amount of energy that one cluster head in UCS spends in one round be E_{ch}. In ECS, the cluster heads in both layers do not spend the same amount of energy during one round. Let the energy spent in one round by a cluster head in layer 1 and layer 2 for ECS be E_{ech1} and E_{ech2}. Then, if the network is dimensioned to last at least T rounds, the cluster head nodes in ECS should be equipped with enough energy to satisfy $E_{B_{ech}} = T \cdot max\{E_{ech1}, E_{ech2}\}$ Joules, assuming that all cluster head nodes have the same batteries. For UCS, cluster head nodes should have batteries with $E_{B_{uch}} = T \cdot E_{ch}$ Joules. We noticed that cluster head nodes in UCS need smaller capacity batteries than cluster head nodes in ECS.

The more balanced energy consumption among the cluster head nodes in UCS comes at a price of more unbalanced energy consumption for the rest of the sensor nodes in the network. In the simplest case, when the network consists of one-hop clusters, the nodes furthest from the cluster head will drain their energy much faster than those closer to the cluster head.

All deployed sensor nodes are of the same type, regardless of the layer to which they belong, and they are equipped with batteries of the same capacity. So, in order that all sensor nodes last during the network lifetime T, with the constraint of equal batteries for all sensors, the batteries of the sensor nodes must be dimensioned as: $E_{sn} = T \cdot E_{fn}$, where E_{fn} is the energy spent in one round by the node in the network that is furthest from its cluster head. Sensor nodes spend energy only to transmit their data to the cluster head, which is equal to: $E_{fni} = c_1 + c_2 \cdot d_{fni}^2$, $i \in \{1, 2\}$, where d_{fni} is the distance of the furthest point to

31

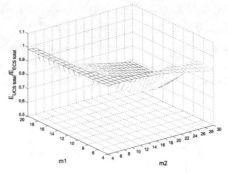

(a) Every cluster head sends 1 aggregated packet.

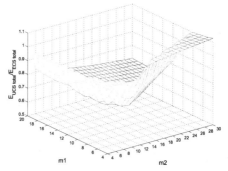

(b) The cluster heads perform aggregation with the efficiency $\alpha = 0.1$.

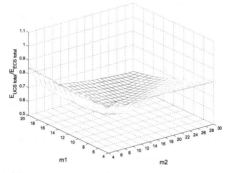

(c) The cluster heads perform aggregation with the efficiency $\alpha = 1$.

Figure 3.3: The ratio of the total energy of batteries for the sensor network organized by the UCS and ECS models.

the cluster head in a cluster for both layers. In order to assure the lifetime T for all sensor nodes, every node has to be equipped with a battery of size $E_{fn} = max\{E_{fn1}, E_{fn2}\}$. The batteries obtained in this way, for both UCS and ECS, are labeled as $E_{B_{usn}}$ and $E_{B_{esn}}$.

We compare the overall energy required for batteries of all nodes in the network, for both UCS and ECS. The total energy needed to assure a lifetime T for all nodes is:

$$E_{UCS_{BT}} = (m_1 + m_2) \cdot E_{B_{uch}} + (N - m_1 - m_2) \cdot E_{B_{usn}} \qquad (3.11)$$

$$E_{ECS_{BT}} = (m_1 + m_2) \cdot E_{B_{ech}} + (N - m_1 - m_2) \cdot E_{B_{esn}} \qquad (3.12)$$

for UCS and ECS, respectively. The ratio of $E_{UCS_{BT}}$ and $E_{ECS_{BT}}$ for different aggregation efficiency parameters is shown in Figure 3.3. On average, the UCS network needs less energy than the ECS network to last during period T without losses. Again, when the network aggregates the data less efficiently, the difference in total energy for ECS and UCS is larger.

3.5   Simulation Results

To validate the analysis from the previous Section, we simulate the performance of the proposed UCS for clustering sensor nodes in a network. Assuming TDMA communication for inter-cluster and intra-cluster communication, we measured the time when the sensor network starts loosing the sensor nodes. The simulations are performed on a network with 400 nodes, randomly deployed over a circular area of radius $R_a = 200m$. We perform simulations for two cases: pie shaped clusters, for which the theoretical analysis was performed in the previous Section, and the more realistic case of Voronoi clusters, where cluster heads are placed in two layers around the base station. The energy that every node spends to transmit a p-bit packet is:

$$E_{tx} = \begin{cases} p \cdot (e_{amf} + e_{fs} \cdot d^2) & d <= d_o \\ p \cdot (e_{amf} + e_{tg} \cdot d^4) & d > d_o \end{cases} \qquad (3.13)$$

where d_o is determined based on the given energy model as $d_o = \sqrt{\frac{e_{fs}}{e_{tg}}}$, with $e_{tg} = 0.0013pJ/bit/m^2$ [48].

3.5.1 Performance of UCS in Heterogeneous Networks

Network Lifetime for UCS and ECS

In the first set of simulations we simulate UCS and ECS in a heterogeneous network. As there are too many parameters to simulate all possible scenarios, for these simulations, we keep the number of cluster heads in layer 1 (m_1) constant while changing the number of clusters in layer 2 (m_2) and varying the radius of the first layer (R_1) in small values from the range $R_1 \in [0.2, 0.9] R_a$. The cluster heads are positioned at the centroids of the clusters, as determined by equations 3.3 and 3.4. The goal is to find, for every pair (m_1, m_2) the maximum number of rounds before the first cluster head in the network dies, and we measure the radius R_1 in that case. This value of R_1 determines the clusters' sizes in layers 1 and 2 that assures the longest lifetime for a particular (m_1, m_2) pair. This algorithm is explained in Figure 3.4.

In these simulations, all cluster head nodes have batteries with the larger energy compared to the batteries of other nodes. Therefore, during the simulations, the sensor nodes start dying after they exhaust their batteries, which affects the number of alive sensors in each cluster over time. Therefore, the simulations provide the more realistic results for the proposed clustering scheme compared to the previous analysis, where we looked into the lifetime of cluster head nodes assuming that all sensor nodes are always alive.

The same set of simulations is repeated for different in-network aggregation coefficients. The final results are obtained by averaging the results of simulations for ten different random scenarios. The results of these simulations are then compared with the simulations of ECS, where the clusters cover approximately the same area and have approximately the same number of nodes.

Figure 3.5 shows the maximum number of rounds the network can last until the first cluster head node in the network dies, for UCS and ECS, when cluster heads forward 10%, 50% and 100% of the cluster load ($\alpha = 0.1, 0.5, 1$). The number of cluster head nodes in the first layer ($m1$) is 6 (Figures 3.5a and 3.5c) and 10 (Figures 3.5b and 3.5d). Using UCS, the sensor network always achieves longer lifetime than with ECS. In most cases, when the maximum number of rounds is reached, the cluster heads spend their energy uniformly over the network. With more clusters closer to the base station, the lifetime of the network improves, as can be seen from Figures 3.5b and 3.5d. For example, when the number of clusters in the first layer is 6, the improvement in lifetime for UCS with the pie shaped scenario is about 10-20%, while when the number of clusters in the first layer increases to 10, the improvement in lifetime is 15-30%, depending on the aggregation efficiency. The

34

```
For m₁ (clusters in the first layer)
    For m₂ (clusters in the second layer)
        For radius R₁, R₁ = [0.2 : 0.05 : 0.9]Rₐ

            Divide network into m₁ + m₂ clusters
            Sizes of clusters are determined by R₁

            Find the positions of cluster head nodes in
            the inner and the outer layer using equations 3.3 and 3.4

            Start simulation:
            Measure t - the maximum number of rounds until the first CH dies
            T(m₁, m₂, R₁) = t

        end
    end
end

For number of clusters in the first layer m₁
    For number of clusters in the second layer m₂
        Find the radius R₁ for which
        T_lifetime(m₁, m₂) = max(T(m₁, m₂, :))
    end
end
```

Figure 3.4: Algorithm used for finding the radius R_1, which determines the sizes of clusters in both layers for which the network achieves the longest lifetime.

improvement with the Voronoi clusters is even higher: 17-35% for $m_1 = 6$, and 15-45% for $m_1 = 10$. Also, the improvement in lifetime increases as the cluster heads perform less aggregation, which confirms that UCS can be useful for heterogeneous networks that perform nonperfect aggregation.

We compare the results for network lifetime obtained in simulations with the network lifetime obtained by considering analysis presented in Section 3.3. Considering different network scenarios we calculated time when the first cluster head in the network dies, while assuming that all sensor nodes are still alive. The network lifetime obtained in this way is shown in Figure 3.6. Figures 3.6a and 3.6b present the network lifetime obtained in the case when the number of the cluster head nodes in the first layer is $m_1 = 6$ and $m_1 = 10$, respectively. These results show that UCS model provides longer network lifetime over ECS model. The network lifetime obtained in this analysis is shorter compared to network lifetime obtained in simulations (given in Figure 3.5), due to the fact that in simulations the sensor nodes start to die after some time. Thus, the cluster head nodes serve less nodes over time, which results in longer network lifetime.

Number of Nodes in UCS Clusters

Figure 3.7 shows the ratio of the average numbers of sensor nodes in the clusters from layers 1 and 2, found by simulations of UCS, for the case when the maximum lifetime of the network is achieved. When the number of cluster head nodes in layer 2 increases, it is observed that the ratio of the number of nodes in the clusters in layer 1 and 2 is slightly smaller. The cluster heads in layer 1 forward more load from the upper layer, so they must support a relatively smaller number of nodes in the cluster.

In general, by comparing the results obtained with pie shape clusters and with Voronoi shaped clusters, we observe similar behaviors. Both scenarios show that UCS can provide the benefit of more uniform energy dissipation for the cluster heads. Also, these results justify our approximation of Voronoi-shaped clusters by pie-shaped clusters used in the previous Section to ease the analysis.

Energy Consumption of Sensor Nodes in UCS and ECS

However, as stated previously, the unequal cluster sizes lead to unequal energy consumption of sensor nodes in a cluster. The average energy consumed by a sensor node per one round in ECS is less than in UCS. Although it is favorable to have less energy consumption of sensor nodes, their ability to send useful data to the base station is determined by the functionality

36

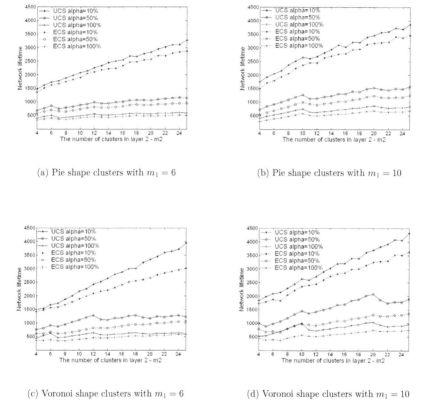

(a) Pie shape clusters with $m_1 = 6$

(b) Pie shape clusters with $m_1 = 10$

(c) Voronoi shape clusters with $m_1 = 6$

(d) Voronoi shape clusters with $m_1 = 10$

Figure 3.5: Maximum number of rounds achieved by the UCS and ECS models.

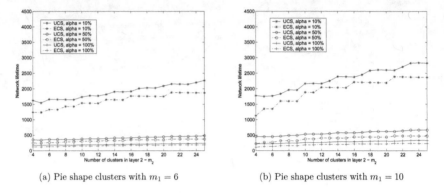

(a) Pie shape clusters with $m_1 = 6$ (b) Pie shape clusters with $m_1 = 10$

Figure 3.6: Maximum number of rounds that can be obtained by UCS and ECS model. These results are calculated based on analysis presented in Section 3.3 and averaged for ten different simulation scenarios.

of cluster heads. To assure that no sensor node runs out of energy before the first cluster head in the network dies, the battery of all sensor nodes should be of size $T \cdot E_{fn}$, where E_{fn} is the energy spent in one round by the node furthest away from its cluster head, and T is the desired number of rounds (network lifetime). Also, for cluster head nodes, the battery should be dimensioned as: $T \cdot max(E_{ch})$, where E_{ch} is the energy spent by a cluster head node in one round.

Using the results from simulations, we dimensioned the batteries of sensor nodes and cluster head nodes, for both ECS and UCS. To achieve the same lifetime in both clustering schemes, the cluster head nodes in UCS should store about 20% less energy than the cluster head nodes in ECS, while the sensor nodes should be equipped with batteries that are about 10-15% larger. Overall, the total energy the network should contain is always smaller for UCS than ECS for the same network lifetime.

These results provide intuition about the use of UCS in a network where all nodes (sensors and cluster heads) have fixed transmission ranges and hence fixed energy dissipation for transmitting data. In this case, the energy consumption of all sensors is the same during one communication round, regardless of their position in the cluster, and thus UCS will always outperform ECS.

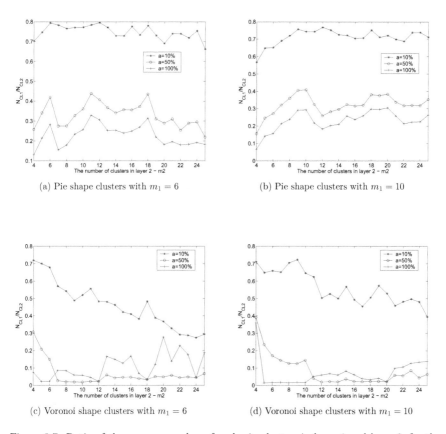

(a) Pie shape clusters with $m_1 = 6$

(b) Pie shape clusters with $m_1 = 10$

(c) Voronoi shape clusters with $m_1 = 6$

(d) Voronoi shape clusters with $m_1 = 10$

Figure 3.7: Ratio of the average number of nodes in clusters in layer 1 and layer 2, for the UCS model.

Heterogeneous Networks with 3 Layers

As a final result for heterogeneous networks, we simulate the same network but now divided it into 3 layers of clusters around the base station. We perform the same type of simulations, where we keep the number of cluster heads in the first layer constant while we change the number of clusters in the second and third layer. Also, we vary the radius of the first and second layers, R_1 and R_2, changing by this the actual cluster sizes in every layer. For every triple (m_1, m_2, m_3) we find the maximum lifetime of the network and the sizes of clusters in that case. Also, we measure the number of rounds the network can last for the cases when the ratio of the number of nodes in clusters of layer 1 and 2, and the ratio of the number of nodes in clusters of layer 2 and 3 is approximately equal to 1. We repeat several simulations on different scenarios, and for different values of the aggregation coefficient α. On average, the improvement in network lifetime when $\alpha = 0.1$ is about 15%, and when $\alpha = 0.5$ and $\alpha = 1$, the improvement is about 26% over ECS.

3.5.2 Performance of UCS in Homogeneous Networks

In this Section, we show the performance of the UCS model applied to a homogeneous sensor network. Since in homogeneous networks all nodes have the same characteristics, in each communication round a certain number of sensor nodes is selected to perform the cluster head roles. The cluster heads route the data over shortest hop paths to the cluster heads closer to the base station.

We perform simulations on two scenarios: first, the network is divided into static clusters, where the nodes are grouped into the same cluster during the network lifetime, and second, when the clustering is dynamic, such that clusters are formed around the elected cluster heads.

3.5.3 Static Homogeneous Clustering

In the first set of simulations, static clusters are formed initially in the early phase of the network, so that every node belongs to one cluster during its lifetime. In every cluster, the role of cluster head is rotated among the nodes, and the cluster head is elected based on maximum remaining energy. Here, we assume that in the initial phase the network is divided into Voronoi-shape clusters, formed around the selected cluster heads and aligned in two layers around the base station. These static clusters with cluster heads that rotate among the cluster nodes can actually be seen as a hybrid solution between the heterogeneous

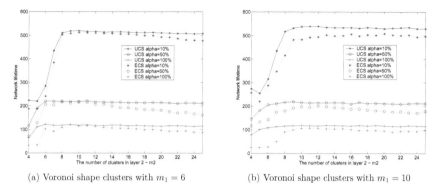

(a) Voronoi shape clusters with $m_1 = 6$ (b) Voronoi shape clusters with $m_1 = 10$

Figure 3.8: Maximum number of rounds achieved by UCS and ECS model, for a network with static clusters.

and homogeneous networks. In static clustering, the large overhead that occurs every time clusters are re-formed can be avoided, which is similar to heterogeneous networks. On the other hand, as in homogeneous networks, the rotation of the cluster head role among the nodes within every cluster contributes to more uniform energy dissipation in the network.

Again, as in the case of heterogeneous networks, we vary the number of clusters in layer 2 (m_2) and the radius of the first layer (R_1) while keeping the number of clusters in layer 1 (m_1) constant. For every set of parameters (m_1, m_2), we measure the maximum network lifetime until 10% of the nodes die, and we determine for which sizes of clusters in both layers this maximum network lifetime is achieved. This network lifetime is compared with the case when all clusters are of approximately the same size (ECS). Figures 3.8a and 3.8b show the maximum number of rounds obtained in simulations of both clustering models, for different numbers of clusters in the inner network layer.

UCS achieves, on average, an 8-28% improvement in network lifetime over ECS, depending on the aggregation efficiency. The improvement is slightly lower than in the case of a heterogeneous network, which is the result of utilizing a static clustering scheme. Although the nodes balance energy better among themselves, all nodes on average perform longer transmissions to the cluster head than in the case when the cluster head is in the middle of the cluster.

It is interesting to observe that for homogeneous networks with static clustering, as the number of clusters in the outer layer increases, the ratio of sizes of clusters of both layers significantly changes, with clusters in layer 1 larger than clusters in layer 2 (Figures 3.9a and

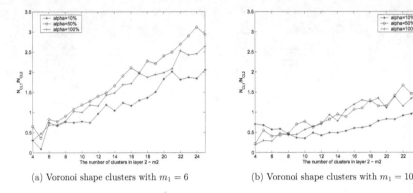

(a) Voronoi shape clusters with $m_1 = 6$ (b) Voronoi shape clusters with $m_1 = 10$

Figure 3.9: The ratio of the average number of nodes in clusters in layers 1 and 2 measured for the UCS model applied to homogeneous sensor networks with static clusters.

3.9b). Because cluster heads in layer 1 receive more packets, they drain their energy faster. Thus, larger clusters in layer 1 assures that there is sufficient energy stored by the larger number of nodes in those clusters, so that one node is not frequently elected for the cluster head position and it does not drain its energy on cluster head activities.

3.5.4 Dynamic Clustering

Finally, we discuss the use of UCS for homogeneous networks utilizing cluster head rotation and dynamic clustering. For these simulations, clusters are formed as Voronoi regions around the elected cluster head nodes.

We compare two clustering models, as the representatives of ECS and UCS. In the first model, all nodes have an equal probability p_o to become cluster head in the next round, where p_o is in the range (0, 0.5]. The sizes of the clusters formed in this manner are not fixed, but the expected number of nodes in every cluster is $\frac{1}{p_o}$. We call this model Equal Probability Election Model (EPEM). For the second case, we again assume that, because of higher energy consumption due to extensive relay activity, the cluster head nodes closer to the base station should support smaller clusters. To obtain smaller clusters in the region around the base station, the nodes in this region have a higher probability of being elected as a cluster head. We call this the Unequal Probability Election Model (UPEM), where the probability of becoming a cluster head for every node depends on the distance d between the node and the base station as:

$$p_i(d) = C \cdot \frac{R_a - d}{R_a}, \tag{3.14}$$

where C is a positive constant.

We compare EPEM and UPEM when the average number of cluster heads elected in every round is the same. In EPEM, the average number of cluster heads elected in every round is simply $k_o = p_o \cdot N$, so the average number of cluster heads in UPEM should be:

$$\frac{N}{R_a^2 \cdot \pi} \int_{R_a}^{0} C \frac{R_a - r}{R_a} \cdot 2\pi r dr = \frac{N \cdot C}{3} = k_o. \tag{3.15}$$

From equation 3.15 the constant C is found as $C = 3 \cdot p_o$.

The probability of node election as a cluster head should satisfy the basic probability condition: $0 \leq p_o \leq 1$, from which we can find a condition for the distance d:

$$d \geq R_a \cdot (1 - \frac{1}{3p_o}). \tag{3.16}$$

Since d is in the range $0 \leq d \leq R_a$, p_o is bounded as:

$$0 \leq p_o \leq \frac{1}{3}. \tag{3.17}$$

When this is not the case, then some nodes closest to the base station should have a probability of being elected as a cluster head equal to 1. This does not, however, mean that they will necessarily serve as a relay station in every round to cluster head nodes further away, because now the nodes further away will have the possibility to choose among more nodes as their next relay station.

The radius R_s, within which all the nodes will have to be chosen as cluster heads with the probability 1, can be determined from the condition that the total number of nodes elected as cluster heads has to be equal to k_o, or:

$$\frac{N}{R_a^2 \pi} \left(\int_0^{R_s} 2\pi r dr + \int_{R_s}^{R_a} 3p_o \frac{R_a - r}{R_a} 2\pi r dr \right) = k_0, \tag{3.18}$$

which gives the value of threshold radius:

$$R_s = R_a \frac{3p_o - 1}{2p_o}. \tag{3.19}$$

Therefore, the probability of cluster head election in UPEM should change as:

43

$$p_i(d) = \begin{cases} 3p_o\frac{R_a-d}{R_a} & 0 \leq d \leq R_a & p_o \leq \frac{1}{3} \\ 1 & 0 \leq d \leq R_s & \frac{1}{3} \leq p_o \leq 1 \\ 3p_o\frac{R_a-d}{R_a} & R_s \leq d \leq R_a & \frac{1}{3} \leq p_o \leq 1 \\ . \end{cases}$$

We compare EPEM and UPEM for several scenarios, changing the probability of cluster head election for EPEM (p_o) and adjusting the probability of cluster head election for UPEM accordingly, for different aggregation coefficients α. Figure 3.10 shows the number of dead nodes during the simulation time.

For the case when p_o is small (Figure 3.10a) and when data is more efficiently aggregated, there is no noticeable difference between EPEM and UPEM. The network has large clusters, and the relay load is not dominant in energy consumption over the energy spent for serving the nodes within the cluster. However, with an increase in relay traffic ($\alpha = 0.5$ and $\alpha = 1$) UPEM performs better than EPEM in terms of the number of nodes that die over the simulation time. The improvement in time until the first node dies in UPEM over EPEM is 23% when $\alpha = 0.5$ and 32% when $\alpha = 1$. The energy spent on load relaying is now dominant, and smaller clusters around the base station can contribute to more uniform energy dissipation.

With an increase in p_o (Figures 3.10b) we can see a difference in the results compared with the case when $p_o = 0.1$. The time until the first node dies is increased with UPEM by 35% for $\alpha = 0.1$, and by 75% for $\alpha = 0.5$ and $\alpha = 1$.

With a further increase in p_o (Figures 3.10c), the network is overloaded with clusters, and with so many data flows the network loses energy quickly. Therefore, the nodes start to die sooner than in the previous cases, but still UPEM achieves significantly better results than EPEM.

3.6 Summary

In this Chapter, we have reviewed our model for hierarchical network organization based on unequal size clusters. We analyzed and compared the performance of this model with the model where the sensor network is divided into equal size clusters. Our unequal size clustering model is designed to better balance the energy consumption of the cluster head sensor nodes, and therefore prolong the lifetime of the network and to prevent the appearance of "hot-spot" areas in the early stages of network lifetime.

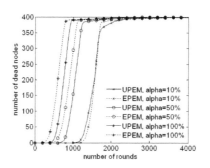

(a) $p_o = 0.1$

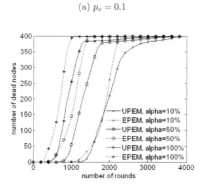

(b) $p_o = 0.3$

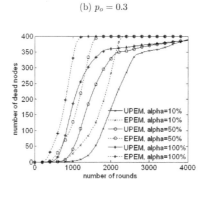

(c) $p_o = 0.5$

Figure 3.10: The number of lost nodes over time for UPEM and EPEM, for different values of probability p_o.

Through the analysis and the extensive simulations of different scenarios for both heterogeneous and homogeneous sensor networks, we showed that our Unequal Cluster Size model can achieve large improvements in network lifetime over the Equal Cluster Size model. A summary of the results of the simulations for different network scenarios is provided in Table 3.1. We notice that the UCS model is especially beneficial in networks where cluster head nodes do not aggregate incoming data significantly, thereby routing large amounts of data through the network.

The general model of having clustered network with clusters of unequal sizes can be applied to other network scenarios. For example, if the base station is further away from the network and in the case of multi-hop inter-cluster routing, the network can be partitioned so that the clusters closer to the base station are much smaller compared to the clusters further away from the base station. However, in the case of direct transmission of data from the cluster head nodes to the base station, the clusters further away should be smaller compared to those clusters closer to the base station, since they spend larger amounts of energy on the direct data transmission to the base station compared to cluster head nodes that are closer to the base station.

Type of Network	Definition of Lifetime	Network Scenario	Improvement of UCS over ECS
Heterogeneous Clusters	First cluster head dies	Pie shaped clusters, $m_1 = 6$	10-20%
		Pie shaped clusters, $m_1 = 10$	15-30%
		Voronoi shaped clusters, $m_1 = 6$	17-35%
		Voronoi shaped clusters, $m_1 = 10$	15-45%
Homogeneous Static Clusters	Time until 10% of nodes die	Voronoi shaped clusters	8-28%
Homogeneous Dynamic Clusters	Time until first node dies	$p_o = 0.1$	23% ($\alpha = 0.5$)
			32% ($\alpha = 1$)
		$p_o = 0.3$	35% ($\alpha = 0.1$)
			75% ($\alpha = 0.5$)
			75% ($\alpha = 1$)

Table 3.1: Summary of simulations results for UCS.

Chapter 4

Coverage-preserving Methods for Cluster Head Selection

In the previous Chapter we discussed ways to balance energy dissipation among the cluster head nodes for heterogeneous sensor networks, or among all the sensor nodes for homogeneous sensor networks. While this is an important goal in many sensor network applications, this approach may not provide maximum lifetime for coverage preservation applications, especially when the sensors are deployed in a nonuniform manner. In applications that require that the monitored region be fully "covered" throughout the network lifetime, it is important to choose cluster head nodes, as well as active sensor and router nodes, so as to preserve coverage as long as possible.

Coverage preservation is one of the basic QoS requirements of wireless sensor networks, yet this problem has not been sufficiently explored in the context of cluster-based sensor networks. Specifically, it is not known how to best select candidates for the cluster head roles in applications that require complete coverage of the monitored area over long periods of time. Oftentimes, the sensor nodes are deployed nonuniformly, so the sensor nodes have different importance to the network coverage task, enabling sensors in redundantly covered areas to sleep more often than nodes in scarcely covered areas without compromising network coverage. In this Chapter, we take a unique look at the cluster head election problem, specifically concentrating on applications where the maintenance of full network coverage is the main requirement. Our approach for cluster-based network organization is based on a set of coverage-aware cost metrics that favor nodes deployed in densely populated network areas as better candidates for cluster head nodes, active sensor nodes and routers. Compared with using traditional energy-based selection methods, using coverage-aware selection of cluster head nodes, active sensor nodes, and routers in a clustered sensor network increases the time during which full coverage of the monitored area can be maintained anywhere from 25% to $4.5x$, depending on the application scenario [59].

4.1 Introduction

Sensor networks oftentimes must provide persistent coverage of the entire monitored area. There are numerous applications where the ability to provide information from each part of the monitored area at any moment is essential for meeting the application's quality of service (QoS). Among these applications are sensor networks for intruder detection and tracking, camera-based surveillance networks, sensor networks for industrial monitoring or actuator sensor networks, for example. In many cases sensors are deployed with much greater density than is needed to satisfy coverage requirements, which enables the redundantly covered nodes to conserve their energy by entering a low-power sleep mode.

While both cluster-based sensor network organization and coverage-maintenance protocols have been extensively studied in the past, these have not been integrated in a coherent manner. Existing techniques for the selection of cluster head nodes base this decision on one of the following: maximum residual energy [18, 60], location of the cluster head candidate relative to the other nodes [61], topology information [19, 62, 63], or previous activity of the sensor node as a cluster head [17]. Although all these approaches contribute to more balanced energy dissipation among the sensor nodes, they do not guarantee coverage for extended periods of time. In other words, energy-balanced clustered network organization does not ensure that the wireless sensor network is able to provide persistent coverage of the entire monitored area. However, sensor coverage is one of the basic network QoS metrics, as it expresses the network's ability to provide constant monitoring/sensing of some area of interest [52, 64]. Therefore, in this Chapter we explore the differences between energy-balanced and coverage-aware sensor network organization, specifically concentrating on clustered wireless sensor networks.

Intuitively, all sensor nodes do not equally contribute to network coverage. The loss of a sensor node deployed in a densely populated area is not as significant for network coverage compared to the loss of nodes from regions that are scarcely populated with sensor nodes. The importance of each sensor node to the coverage preserving task can be quantitatively expressed by a *coverage-aware* cost metric, which is a metric originally introduced in [44]. This cost metric considers the node's remaining energy as well as the coverage redundancy of its sensing range, thereby measuring the contribution of this node to the network's coverage task.

In this Chapter we analyze how different coverage-aware cost metrics, some of which were defined in [44], can be utilized in the periodic election of cluster head nodes, ensuring that sensors that are important to the coverage task are less likely to be selected as cluster head nodes. Furthermore, the same coverage-aware cost metrics are used to find the set of active sensor nodes that provide full coverage, as well as the set of routers that forward the cluster head nodes' data load to the sink. We show the benefits of using this coverage-aware approach compared to traditional energy-based clustering by comparing our approach with HEED [18] for coverage-preserving applications. Our results show clearly that clustering in sensor networks should be directed by two fundamental requirements—energy conservation and coverage preservation.

4.2   Family of Coverage-Aware Cost Metrics

The DAPR (Distributed Activation with Predetermined Routes) protocol proposed in [44] is the first routing protocol designed to avoid routing of data through areas sparsely covered by the sensor nodes. The idea behind this approach is that the use of nodes in sparsely deployed areas, as well as the use of nodes with small remaining energies, as data routers should be minimized, so that these nodes can collect data for longer periods of time. To accomplish this goal, the importance of every sensor node for the coverage preserving task is quantified by a *coverage-aware* cost metric, which combines the information about the node's remaining energy with information about how redundantly this node's sensing area is covered by its neighboring nodes' sensing areas.

To explore the benefit of this approach in cluster-based sensor networks, we introduce several coverage-aware cost metrics. We assume that N_s sensor nodes from a set S, $s_i \in S$, $i = 1..N_s$ are scattered randomly over a rectangular monitored area A. We assume the application requires that every part of the scene be covered by the sensors throughout the network lifetime. Each sensor performs reliable sensing within its sensing area $C(s_i)$, which is approximated by a circular area around the node with radius R_{sense}. Note that this is a simple model for sensor coverage. Other techniques such as utilizing a learning phase where sensors learn their sensing area $C(s_i)$ based on training data can be used as well.

For every sensor node s_i we define a group of neighboring nodes $N(i)$ that includes all nodes with sensing areas either partially or fully overlapped with the sensing area of node

s_i. Using our model for sensing area, we obtain:

$$N(i) = \{s_j \mid d(s_i, s_j) \le 2 \cdot R_{sense}\}, \tag{4.1}$$

where $d(s_i, s_j)$ is the Euclidean distance between nodes s_i and s_j.

To reduce the number of active nodes while ensuring that every point (x, y) of the monitored region is covered by at least one sensor, each node needs to determine the overlap of its sensing area with the sensing areas of its neighboring nodes. For this, we assume that sensor nodes have localization capabilities. Considering each node's position and its residual energy, for each point (x, y) of the monitored area A we define the total energy $E_{total}(x, y)$ that is available for monitoring that location:

$$E_{total}(x, y) = \sum_{s_j:(x,y) \in C(s_j)} E(s_j), \tag{4.2}$$

where $E(s_j)$ is the remaining energy of node s_j.

The first two cost metrics presented below, and defined in [44], are based on the total energy $E_{total}(x, y)$ available for monitoring each location in the sensor field.

4.2.1   Minimum Weight Coverage Cost

The minimum-weight coverage cost is defined as:

$$C_{mw}(s_i) = \max \frac{1}{E_{total}(x, y)}, \qquad (x, y) \in C(s_i) \tag{4.3}$$

This cost metric measures node s_i's importance for the network coverage task by considering the energy of the most critically covered location (x, y) within the sensing area of the node.

4.2.2   Weighted Sum Coverage Cost

The weighted-sum coverage cost is defined as:

$$C_{ws}(s_i) = \int_{C(s_i)} \frac{dxdy}{E_{total}(x, y)} = \int_{C(s_i)} \frac{dxdy}{\sum_{s_j:(x,y) \in C(s_j)} E(s_j)}. \tag{4.4}$$

This cost metric measures the weighted average of the total energies of all points that are covered by the sensing area of node s_i.

4.2.3 Coverage Redundancy Cost

The coverage redundancy cost metric does not depend on a node's remaining energy nor on the remaining energies of its neighbors. Instead, this cost considers only the coverage redundancy of the overlapped sensing areas between the sensor and its neighboring nodes. Similarly to the previously defined $E_{total}(x,y)$, we define a total coverage $O_{total}(x,y)$, which reflects the number of nodes that cover each point (x,y) of the area A:

$$O_{total}(x,y) = \sum_{s_j:(x,y)\in C(s_j)} 1. \qquad (4.5)$$

Then, the coverage redundancy cost of sensor s_i is:

$$C_{cc}(s_i) = \int_{C(s_i)} \frac{dxdy}{O_{total}(x,y)} = \int_{C(s_i)} \frac{dxdy}{\sum_{s_j:(x,y)\in C(s_j)} 1}. \qquad (4.6)$$

Figure 4.1 provides an example that illustrates the minimum-weight, weighted-sum and coverage redundancy cost metrics. This example considers three nodes s_1, s_2 and s_3 with remaining energies $E(s_1)$, $E(s_2)$ and $E(s_3)$. The parameters A_i, $A_{i,j}$ and A_{ijk}, $i,j,k \in \{1,2,3\}$ are the areas of overlapped portions of the nodes' sensing areas.

4.2.4 Energy-aware Cost

The energy-aware cost function evaluates the sensor's ability to take part in the sensing task based solely on its remaining energy $E(s_i)$:

$$C_{ea}(s_i) = \frac{1}{E(s_i)}. \qquad (4.7)$$

4.2.5 Coverage-aware Routing Cost

The cost metrics introduced in the previous subsections are the basis for *coverage-aware routing*, where the minimum cost routing paths are determined such that high cost nodes are excluded from the routing task. The cost of a link between two nodes s_i and s_j is equal to the energy spent by these nodes to transmit $(E_{tx}(s_i, s_j))$ and to receive $(E_{rx}(s_i, s_j))$ one data packet, weighted by the costs of these nodes:

$$C_{link}(s_i, s_j) = C_{aa}(s_i) \cdot E_{tx}(s_i, s_j) + C_{aa}(s_j) \cdot E_{rx}(s_i, s_j), \qquad (4.8)$$

where C_{aa} represents any of the cost metrics described above. Therefore, the minimum cumulative cost path from each node to the sink is found as:

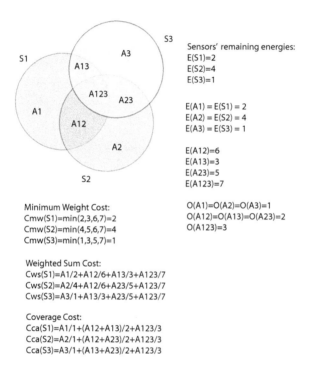

Sensors' remaining energies:
E(S1)=2
E(S2)=4
E(S3)=1

E(A1) = E(S1) = 2
E(A2) = E(S2) = 4
E(A3) = E(S3) = 1

E(A12)=6
E(A13)=3
E(A23)=5
E(A123)=7

O(A1)=O(A2)=O(A3)=1
O(A12)=O(A13)=O(A23)=2
O(A123)=3

Minimum Weight Cost:
Cmw(S1)=min(2,3,6,7)=2
Cmw(S2)=min(4,5,6,7)=4
Cmw(S3)=min(1,3,5,7)=1

Weighted Sum Cost:
Cws(S1)=A1/2+A12/6+A13/3+A123/7
Cws(S2)=A2/4+A12/6+A23/5+A123/7
Cws(S3)=A3/1+A13/3+A23/5+A123/7

Coverage Cost:
Cca(S1)=A1/1+(A12+A13)/2+A123/3
Cca(S2)=A2/1+(A12+A23)/2+A123/3
Cca(S3)=A3/1+(A13+A23)/2+A123/3

Figure 4.1: Illustration of the coverage-aware cost metrics.

$$C_{final}(s_i) = \sum_{s_j,s_k \in p(s_i,S_{dst})} C_{link}(s_j,s_k), \qquad (4.9)$$

where p is the minimum cost path from node s_i to the sink S_{dst}. The cost defined by equation 4.9 is called the coverage-aware routing cost.

Data routing from every cluster head to the sink is done over multi-hop paths, which are found by minimizing C_{final} in equation 4.9. More details about routing from the cluster head nodes to the data sink are provided in Section 4.3.

4.3   Coverage Preserving Clustering Protocol (CPCP)

To ensure balanced energy consumption among the cluster head nodes throughout the network lifetime, many clustering protocols favor uniformly distributed clusters with stable average cluster sizes. However, obtaining the same number of well distributed clusters over time is a real challenge in clustered sensor networks.

In coverage-based applications, the best candidates for cluster head roles should be the redundantly covered nodes in densely populated areas with high remaining energy. These nodes can support clusters with a large number of members. While the excessive energy consumption of the cluster head nodes makes these nodes die before the other nodes, since they are located in densely populated areas, their death should not affect the overall network coverage. Using our approach, which considers the application's requirements for full network coverage, the set of cluster head nodes can be selected based on the cost metrics defined in Section 4.2. However, cluster head selection based solely on any of the proposed cost metrics using existing clustering techniques will lead to an undesirable situation: the densely populated parts of the network will be overcrowded with cluster head nodes, while the scarcely covered areas will be left without any cluster head nodes. In such a situation, it is likely that the high cost sensors from poorly covered areas will have the additional burden of performing expensive data transmissions to distant cluster head nodes, further reducing their lifetime.

In order to avoid this situation, we propose the clustering method called Coverage Preserving Clustering Protocol (CPCP). CPCP spreads cluster head nodes more uniformly throughout the network by limiting the maximum cluster area. Thus, clusters in sparsely covered areas are formed as well as clusters in densely covered areas, which prevents the high cost nodes from having to perform costly packet transmissions to distant cluster head nodes.

Also, nodes from the sparsely covered areas elected to serve as cluster head nodes support clusters with a smaller number of nodes compared to cluster head nodes in dense areas.

We define the cluster radius $R_{cluster}$ as a tunable parameter that determines the minimum distance between any two cluster head nodes in the network. Using this parameter, CPCP prevents the appearance of nonuniformly distributed clusters within the network. $R_{cluster}$ can be easily tuned by changing the transmission power of the cluster head nodes.

In CPCP the sensor nodes communicate directly with their elected cluster head nodes, while data routing from the cluster head nodes to the sink is done over multi-hop paths using the sensors. CPCP consists of six phases: information update, cluster head election, route update, cluster formation, sensor activation and data communication, as described below.

4.3.1 Phase I: Information Update

The first phase of CPCP is reserved for updating information on the remaining energies of the nodes. Each sensor node broadcasts an update packet with information about its remaining energy to all its neighbors in the range $2 \cdot R_{sense}$. In order to reduce packet collisions, the nodes use random back-offs before sending the update packets. Upon receiving the update information from all neighbors, each node calculates its coverage-aware cost, as described previously. Assuming that the sensor nodes are static, the neighboring nodes must exchange their location information only once, at the beginning of the network lifetime.

If the coverage redundancy cost or the energy-aware cost are used, then this Information Update phase can be skipped, since these cost metrics do not depend on the neighboring nodes' remaining energies.

4.3.2 Phase II: Cluster Head Election

At the beginning of this phase every sensor determines its "activation time"—an amount of time proportional to its cost. Each sensor has to wait for the expiration of its "activation time" before deciding weather or not it should announce itself as a new cluster head for the upcoming communication round. If during the "activation time" a node does not hear an announcement message from any other sensor node, then, upon expiration of its "activation time" it declares itself a new cluster head, by sending an announcement message to all the nodes within the $R_{cluster}$ range. The announcement message contains information about the node's location.

After receiving an announcement message from a new cluster head node, all nodes in $R_{cluster}$ range exclude themselves from further consideration for the cluster head role. Each

Algorithm 1 The cluster head election and cluster formation phases of CPCP.

1: $S = \{s \mid E(s) > 0\}$, $E(s)$ $-residual\ energy\ of\ node\ s$
2: $S_{CH} = \{\}$
3: $T_{ch}(i) = \{\}, i = 1..N$
4: **while** $S \notin \{\}$ **do**
5:    $(s_k - node\ with\ minimum\ cost)$ & $(E(s_k) > E_{th})$
6:    $S_{CH} = S_{CH} \cup s_k$
7:    $N(k) = \{s \mid dist(s, s_k) < R_{cluster}\}$
8:    $\forall s \in N(k), T_{ch}(s) = T_{ch}(s) \cup s_k$
9:    $S = S \setminus N(k)$
10: **end while**
11: $\forall s \mid S_{CH} \cap s = \{\varnothing\}$
12: s $sends$ $JOIN$ $message$ to $cluster$ $head$ s_{CH} for $which$ $dist(s, s_{CH}) = min(dist(s, s_i)), \forall s_i \in T_{ch}(s)$
13: $S_{un} = \{s \mid (S_{ch}(s) = \{\varnothing\})$ & $(S_{CH} \cup s = \{\varnothing\})\}$
14: **if** $S_{un} \notin \{\}$ **then**
15:    $\forall s \in S_{un}, find\ s_n \mid dist(s, s_n) = min(dist(s, s_i)), \forall s_i \in N(s)$
16:    s $sends$ $data$ $packet$ to s_n
17: **end if**

sensor node maintains a table of all cluster head nodes from which it has received the announcement message so far, as well as the distance to each cluster head node. This information is used later by the node to decide about its cluster membership. Rarely it may happen that two nodes with the same costs and within each other's $R_{cluster}$ range simultaneously declare themselves to be new cluster head nodes — this conflict can be solved by giving priority to the node with the higher remaining energy.

When cost metrics C_{mw}, C_{ws} or C_{cc} are used, it can happen that a node with low remaining energy is elected to serve as a cluster head. This may cause the loss of the cluster's data during the communication round. This outcome can be avoided by preventing those nodes that have remaining energy below a certain threshold E_{th} from taking part in the cluster head election process. If, after the cluster head election phase, these nodes do not belong to any of the elected cluster head nodes, they find the nearest sensor node to which they forward their data. The pseudo code for the cluster head election phase of CPCP is provided in Algorithm 1.

4.3.3   Phase III: Route Update

The cluster head nodes send their data over multi-hop paths to the sink. To obtain these routes, the sink node first generates a *Route Discovery* message that is broadcasted throughout the network. Upon receiving the broadcast message, each node introduces a delay proportional to its cost before it forwards the *Route Discovery* message. In this way a message arrives at each node along the desired minimum cost path. The cumulative cost of the routing path from the sink to the node obtained in this phase is called the *coverage-aware routing cost* of the node, as described in equation 4.9.

4.3.4   Phase IV: Cluster Formation

In the fourth phase of CPCP, each node decides to join the closest cluster head node. The nodes send short *JOIN* messages to their selected cluster head nodes. These *JOIN* messages serve as an acknowledgement that a node will become a member of the cluster for the upcoming round. In this way, selected cluster head nodes form Voronoi-shaped clusters as shown in Figure 4.2.

4.3.5   Phase V: Sensor Activation

In the fifth phase, a subset of sensor nodes is selected to perform the sensing task for the upcoming round, while the rest of the nodes go to sleep. The selected active nodes provide full coverage over the monitored field during this communication round.

In the Sensor Activation phase, each sensor node assigns itself an activation delay that is inversely proportional to its current application cost. Each node then waits for this period of time before deciding whether it will stay awake during the next communication round. If, after its activation delay time expires, the sensor node determines that its sensing area is completely covered by its neighboring nodes, it turns itself off for the upcoming round. Otherwise, the sensor node broadcasts an acknowledgement message to inform its neighbors about its decision to remain active. In this way, the higher cost nodes have priority to decide whether they should be active. All nodes in the network jointly take part in the activation phase, regardless of the cluster to which they belong. This eliminates the redundant activation of sensor nodes on the borders of the clusters, which may happen when the activation of nodes is done in each cluster independently.

4.3.6 Phase VI: Data Communication

Once clusters are formed and active sensors are selected, the Data Communication phase begins where the active sensor nodes periodically collect data and send it to the cluster head nodes. The cluster head nodes aggregate the data from the cluster members, and route the aggregated data packets over the pre-determined multi-hop paths to the sink.

4.4 Simulation Set-up

In this Section we discuss the set-up for our simulations that measure the performance of CPCP. In all the simulations we measure the percentage of the area covered by the active sensor nodes over time. Since active nodes selected in the Activation Phase of CPCP maximally cover the monitored area, the measured coverage provided by these active nodes is the same as the coverage that would be provided by all alive nodes in the network.

We perform two sets of simulations. In the first set of simulations, we compare the performance of CPCP using the different cost metrics introduced in Section 4.2 for the selection of cluster head nodes, active sensors and routers. In the second set of simulations, we compare CPCP with the HEED clustering protocol as a representative of the many energy-aware clustering protocols. Furthermore, in our simulations we vary the amount of data aggregation and the network scenario, as described next, to determine the performance of CPCP over a wide range of conditions.

4.4.1 Data Aggregation

In many applications, the cluster head nodes aggregate the received data, thereby reducing the total energy required for transmitting data back to the sink. The amount of aggregated data produced by the cluster head nodes depends on the data aggregation algorithm as well as on the application requirements and the type of sensor data. In our simulations, we provide results for scenarios when the cluster head nodes aggregate their received data more or less efficiently, meaning that they provide different numbers of aggregated data packets. In particular, we present results of simulations where the cluster head nodes aggregate all data into a single outgoing packet, as well as when they reduce the amount of collected data by half, and when the aggregated data is 80% of the total data load collected within the cluster.

Parameter	Acronym	Value
Tx/Rx electronics constant [17]	E_{amp}	$50nJ/bit$
Amplifier constant [17]	ϵ_{fs}	$10pJ/bit/m^2$
Path-loss exponent	n	2
CH energy threshold	E_{th}	$10^{-4}J$
Packet size	p	$30bytes$
Packet rate	B	$1packet/s$
Maximum transmission range	r_{tx}	70m
Sensing range	R_{sense}	15m
Cluster range	$R_{cluster}$	30m

Table 4.1: Simulation parameters for CPCP.

4.4.2 Network Scenario

We conduct simulations for two scenarios: a network with 200 nodes deployed over an area of size $100 \times 100m^2$, and a network with 400 nodes deployed over an area of size $200 \times 200m^2$. The nodes are deployed either randomly or nonuniformly. In the case of the random deployment, the locations of sensor nodes are randomly chosen based on the random-uniform distribution. For simplicity, we call this deployment the *random* deployment. The nonuniform deployment corresponds to the case when nodes in certain parts of the network are more "grouped" together, meaning that they provide higher redundancy in coverage than the nodes located in scarcely covered areas of the network. We call this deployment the *nonuniform* deployment. The data sink is fixed and located in the center of the network. The simulations are conducted with $R_{cluster} = 2 \cdot R_{sense}$. The simulation parameters are summarized in Table 4.1.

4.4.3 Energy Model

We assume that the sensor nodes have the ability to adjust their transmission power according to the distance of the receiving node. We use the free-space energy model defined in [17], where the energies required to transmit and to receive a p-bit packet are given by equations 3.1 and 3.2, respectively. All simulation parameters are listed in Table 4.1.

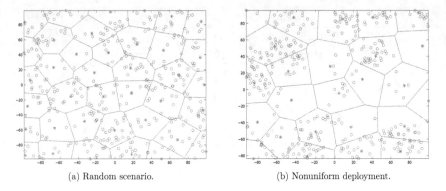

(a) Random scenario.   (b) Nonuniform deployment.

Figure 4.2: Examples of random and nonuniform deployment scenarios. CPCP achieves uniform distribution of the cluster head nodes.

4.4.4   Clusters Created Using CPCP

Simulations show that CPCP disperses cluster head nodes uniformly, as shown in Figure 4.2, thereby producing small variations in the number of cluster head nodes elected in successive communication rounds. Thus, in the case of the random deployment scenario (Figure 4.2a), the data load produced in the network is more uniformly distributed across the cluster head nodes over time. In the case of the nonuniform scenario (Figure 4.2b) the cluster head nodes in redundantly covered areas serve clusters with a higher number of nodes than the cluster head nodes in sparsely covered network areas. However, sensor nodes in densely populated network areas are less critical to the coverage task, which enables these nodes to spend more energy by serving clusters with larger numbers of nodes, without degrading network coverage.

Figure 4.3 shows the average number of cluster head nodes per round as well as the standard deviation of the average number of active nodes per cluster over the time period during which the network provides full coverage of the monitored area. For both scenarios (random and nonuniform) the variations in the number of cluster head nodes per round over time are small. The number of cluster head nodes is lower in the nonuniform deployment scenarios due to the existence of larger areas with very low densities of sensor nodes. Also, when the network is deployed in a nonuniform manner, the standard deviation in the average number of active nodes is slightly higher than in case of random deployment, as shown in Figures 4.3b and 4.3d.

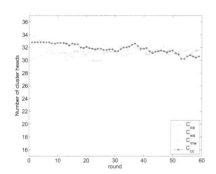

(a) Average number of cluster head nodes per round, random scenario.

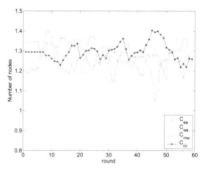

(b) Standard deviation of the average number of active nodes per cluster, random scenario.

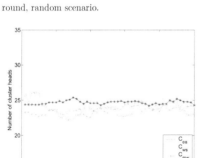

(c) Average number of cluster head nodes per round, nonuniform scenario.

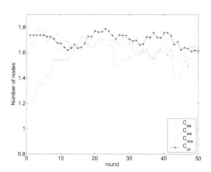

(d) Standard deviation of the average number of active nodes per cluster, nonuniform scenario.

Figure 4.3: Performance of CPCP: the average number of cluster head nodes per round and the standard deviation of the average number of active nodes per cluster when the network is operating at 100% coverage.

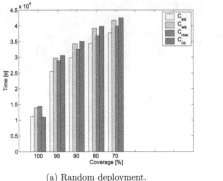 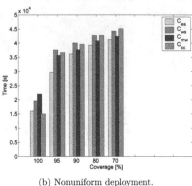

(a) Random deployment.   (b) Nonuniform deployment.

Figure 4.4: Coverage-time for a network of size $100 \times 100m^2$ with 200 nodes utilizing CPCP with different cost metrics.

4.5 Case I: Performance of CPCP Using Different Cost Metrics

Our goal with this first set of simulations is to show the effects of the different cost metrics on the performance of the network, specifically focusing on coverage-time. These costs are used to select cluster head nodes, active sensors and routing nodes. The cluster head nodes aggregate the data packets received from the active sensors within the cluster into one outgoing packet, and this packet is routed to the sink via shortest-cost routes determined in the Route Update phase.

4.5.1 Time vs. Coverage as the Network Scales

First we find the coverage-time using the different cost metrics as the network scales from $100 \times 100m^2$ with 200 sensor nodes to $200 \times 200m^2$ with 400 sensor nodes for both random and nonuniform deployment scenarios. The results for the network of size $100 \times 100m^2$ with 200 sensor nodes are shown in Figure 4.4. When the selection of cluster head nodes, active nodes and routers is done using the minimum-weight cost (C_{mw}) and the weighted-sum cost (C_{ws}), the improvement in the time during which the randomly deployed network can provide full coverage (100%) over the energy-aware cost (C_{ea}) is 30% and 22%, respectively (Figure 4.4a). For the nonuniform scenario, these improvements of coverage-time increase to 38% and 25%, respectively (Figure 4.4b). After the network coverage drops below 95%,

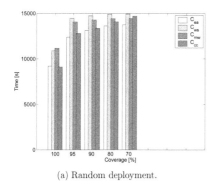

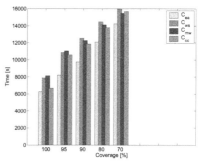

(a) Random deployment.

(b) Nonuniform deployment.

Figure 4.5: Coverage-time for a network of size $200 \times 200m^2$ with 400 nodes utilizing CPCP with different cost metrics.

C_{mw} and C_{ws} improve the coverage-time by $15 - 20\%$ in the case of random deployment, and by $20 - 25\%$ in the case of nonuniform deployment. Overall, these two metrics are able to provide longer coverage-time over C_{ea} in both the random and nonuniform network deployment scenarios.

Figure 4.5 shows the results of the simulations for the larger network ($200 \times 200m^2$ with 400 nodes). Again, the C_{mw} and C_{ws} metrics provide longer coverage-time compared to the C_{ea} metric. The improvement in the coverage-time is higher in the nonuniform deployment scenario, with an improvement in coverage-time for 100% coverage of 28% using C_{mw} and 26% using C_{ws}. The minimum-weight cost C_{mw} again provides the longest time during which 100% of the network is covered compared to all the other cost metrics in both the random (Figure 4.5a) and nonuniform (Figure 4.5b) network deployments. This is expected, since the minimum-weight cost assigns a high cost to the nodes that are critical to maintaining 100% coverage.

Compared with the other metrics, the coverage redundancy cost metric (C_{cc}) provides the worst time during which the network is able to monitor the entire (100%) area, which is the main QoS requirement of the coverage-preserving application. However, in the case of smaller networks ($100 \times 100m^2$), after the coverage starts to drop below 80%, C_{cc} shows slightly better performance than the other cost metrics. In the larger network ($200 \times 200m^2$), C_{cc} always performs worse than C_{ws} cost metric. The difference in the results obtained with the coverage redundancy metric for both simulated scenarios (small and large network) illustrates the importance of applying the same coverage-aware approach in the selection

63

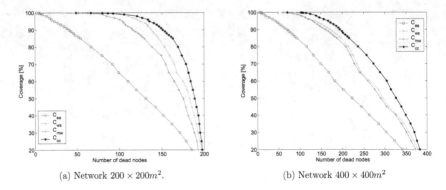

(a) Network $200 \times 200m^2$.　　　　　　　　(b) Network $400 \times 400m^2$

Figure 4.6: Network coverage as a function of the number of dead nodes.

of not only cluster head nodes, but also in the selection of data routers as well. With the increase of network size, routing is done over a larger number of hops; therefore, there is a greater need to avoid the critical nodes (non-redundantly covered nodes or nodes with low energy). Although the coverage-redundancy cost metric selects redundantly covered nodes, it does not consider the node's remaining energy, resulting more often in the loss of nodes compared with the other metrics. In the case of smaller networks, this is less evident than in the case of larger networks, which is one reason that the coverage-redundancy cost metric never outperforms the other metrics.

To explain these simulation results further, we performed further experiments to provide more details about the clusters and routes that are found using the different cost metrics, described next.

4.5.2　Loss of Sensor Nodes

Figure 4.6 shows how the network coverage decreases as the number of dead nodes increases for the two network scenarios ($100 \times 100m^2$ with 200 nodes and $200 \times 200m^2$ with 400 nodes). The C_{ea} cost metric contributes to uniform energy dissipation among the sensor nodes, resulting in the highest amount of lost coverage for a given number of dead nodes compared to the other three metrics. On the other hand, the coverage redundancy cost metric has the least amount of coverage loss for a given number of dead nodes. This shows that the energy-aware cost metric treats all nodes equally, while the coverage redundancy cost metric preserves nodes that are critical for the coverage task. As the coverage redundancy cost

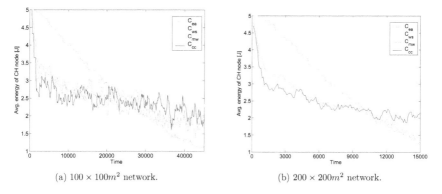

(a) $100 \times 100m^2$ network.   (b) $200 \times 200m^2$ network.

Figure 4.7: Remaining energy levels of selected cluster head nodes over time.

metric does not consider a node's remaining energy, a node's cost only changes when one of its neighboring nodes dies. This infrequent change in node cost results in non-balanced energy consumption, with the result that redundantly covered sensors that are not critical to the coverage of the network, are used first.

Coverage as a function of the number of dead nodes using the other two cost metrics (C_{mw} and C_{ws}) is in between that of C_{ea} and C_{cc}. Note, however, that C_{mw} and C_{ws} provide the longest coverage-time compared to the other two metrics. This clearly demonstrates the fact that it is important to look at *both* minimizing or balancing energy dissipation and preserving critical nodes to maintain high levels of coverage for a longer time.

Figure 4.7 shows the average energy of the selected cluster head nodes over time. When C_{ea} is used, sensor nodes with the highest remaining energy are selected as cluster head nodes. Compared to using the C_{ea} cost, using the C_{mw} and C_{ws} cost metrics prevent non-redundantly covered nodes from being selected as cluster head nodes at the beginning of the network lifetime, resulting in rotation of cluster head roles among the most redundantly covered sensor nodes. The frequent selection and excessive energy consumption of elected cluster head nodes using the C_{mw} and C_{ws} costs lead to loss of the most redundantly covered nodes. At that point, the low redundantly covered sensor nodes resume the cluster head roles and, since they have not yet served as cluster heads previously, these nodes still have relatively high remaining energies. This is the reason why at a certain point, after the network coverage using the C_{ea} cost drops below 95% (by comparing Figures 4.4b and 4.7a, and Figures 4.5b and 4.7b) the average energy of elected cluster head nodes using C_{mw} and C_{ws} is larger than the average energy of cluster head nodes elected using the C_{ea} metric.

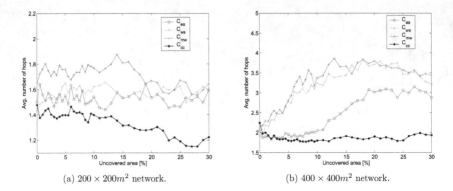

(a) $200 \times 200m^2$ network.   (b) $400 \times 400m^2$ network.

Figure 4.8: Average number of hops in the routes from the cluster head nodes to the sink.

4.5.3 Coverage-aware Routing

Figure 4.8 shows the average number of hops in the routes from the cluster head nodes to the sink as the network coverage changes. These results show that the C_{cc} cost metric finds routes with the smallest number of hops compared with the other cost metrics. On the other hand, the weighted-sum (C_{ws}) and minimum-weight (C_{mw}) metrics route data packets over the the longest paths, since these metrics try to avoid the high cost nodes (those with low remaining energy and/or with low redundancy in coverage). In the case of the smaller networks ($100 \times 100m^2$, shown in Figure 4.8a), data packets are routed over a relatively small number of hops (1 to 2), so the differences in the average path lengths for the various cost metrics are not significant. Therefore, the choice of routing paths does not significantly affect the network performance.

However, in the case of the larger networks ($200 \times 200m^2$), the differences in the lengths of the routing paths are more evident for different costs, as shown in Figure 4.8b. As network coverage decreases, the minimum-weight and weighted-sum metrics further increase the number of hops in their routing paths, trying to avoid critical nodes. When the coverage of the network starts to decrease as a result of losing nodes, the energy-aware metric also increases the average number of hops in order to balance energy dissipation throughout the network, whereas the coverage redundancy cost keeps route lengths fairly constant.

As a result of the increased lengths of the routing paths, the average energy dissipated to route packets from each cluster head node to the sink also increases for the C_{mw}, C_{ws} and C_{ea} cost metrics, as illustrated in Figure 4.9. Again, in the large networks, this increase in

66

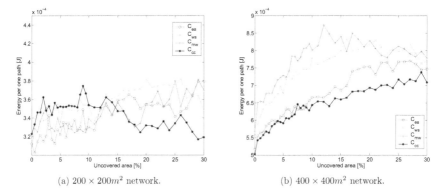

(a) $200 \times 200 m^2$ network.   (b) $400 \times 400 m^2$ network.

Figure 4.9: Average energy dissipated per route from the cluster head nodes to the sink.

average energy dissipation per path is more evident than in the case of the smaller networks.

The coverage redundancy cost C_{cc} does not prevent routing over the low-energy nodes, which speeds up the loss of these nodes. The average number of hops used for data routing is small, and it stays relatively constant throughout the network lifetime (Figure 4.8). Using C_{cc} the average energy spent per route is smaller compared to other cost metrics, once the network starts loosing coverage (Figure4.9). The reason for this is that the network loses a significant number of nodes, which reduces the total data load routed through the network. In the case of the smaller networks, where data are routed over a small number of hops, this is the reason that C_{cc} starts to outperform the other cost metrics when the network's coverage starts to decrease significantly. However, when data are routed over a larger number of hops, C_{cc} shows an inability to choose "good" routing paths, which is the reason this cost metric does not perform well. This again illustrates the importance of considering both energy and coverage in the selection of routing paths for coverage-preserving applications.

4.5.4   Increasing the Number of Nodes

Figure 4.10 shows the time during which the $200 \times 200 m^2$ networks provide 100% coverage when the number of nodes increases from 200 to 600, for both the random and nonuniform deployments. In all cases the C_{ws} and C_{mw} cost metrics provide longer network coverage-time compared to the C_{ea} cost metric. The improvements in network coverage time obtained with the C_{ws} and C_{mw} cost metrics compared with the C_{ea} cost metric in the nonuniform network deployment scenarios is always larger than in the random network deployments. Therefore,

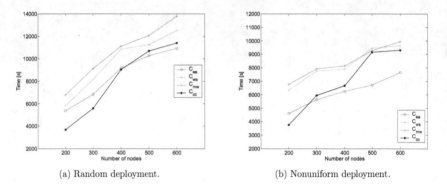

(a) Random deployment. (b) Nonuniform deployment.

Figure 4.10: Time during which the network preserves 100% coverage of the monitored area as a function of the number of nodes in the $200 \times 200m^2$ network.

the advantages of using minimum-weight and weighted sum cost metrics over energy-aware cost are even more evident in the nonuniform sensor network deployment scenarios.

4.5.5 Impact of Data Aggregation

When cluster head nodes perform less efficient data aggregation, meaning that they send more than one packet to the sink, the differences in coverage-time obtained by the coverage-aware cost metrics and the energy-aware cost metric increase. Figure 4.11 shows the coverage-time obtained with different cost metrics when the cluster head nodes forward 50% and 80% of all packets received from the cluster members in one communication round. In both cases the C_{mw} and C_{ws} cost metrics perform even better compared to the C_{ea} metric than in the case when the cluster head aggregates all incoming data into one packet. The improvement in the time during which the network provides 100% coverage using C_{ws} and C_{mw} compared with using C_{ea} is $2.5x$ and $3.2x$, respectively, when the cluster heads forward half of the total received data. When the cluster heads forward 80% of the total received load, these improvements are even higher—$3.6x$ using C_{ws} and $4.5x$ using C_{mw} compared with using the C_{ea} cost metric.

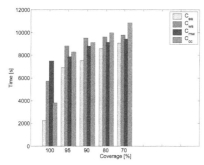
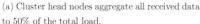
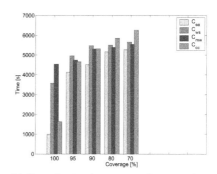

(a) Cluster head nodes aggregate all received data to 50% of the total load.

(b) Cluster head nodes aggregate all received data to 80% of the total load.

Figure 4.11: The effect of aggregation efficiency on coverage-time for the $200 \times 200m^2$ network with 400 nonuniformly deployed nodes.

4.6 Case II: Performance of CPCP Compared with HEED

As mentioned previously, many clustering protocols are mainly focused on achieving balanced energy consumption in the network in order to prolong the lifetime of the individual sensor nodes, without regard to the network's ability to cover the region of interest. In order to illustrate the difference between coverage-preserving and energy balancing approaches to cluster organization, we compare CPCP with the HEED protocol [18]. HEED is a scalable protocol that achieves balanced energy consumption among the sensor nodes, and it provides uniform distribution of cluster head nodes throughout the network, which significantly prolongs the network lifetime.

4.6.1 Overview of HEED

HEED (Hybrid Energy-Efficient Distributed clustering) is an iterative clustering protocol that uses information about the nodes' remaining energy and their communication costs in order to select the best set of cluster head nodes. During the clustering process, a sensor node can be either a tentative cluster head, a final cluster head, or it can be covered (meaning that it has heard an announcement message from a final cluster head node). At the beginning of the clustering phase, a node with higher remaining energy has a higher probability CH_{prob} of becoming a tentative cluster head. If the node becomes a tentative cluster head, it broadcasts a message to all sensor nodes within its cluster range to announce its new status. All nodes that hear from at least one tentative cluster head choose their cluster head nodes based on the costs of the tentative cluster head nodes. For this purpose, the authors in [18] define the *average reachability power* ($AMRP$), which is a cost metric used to "break ties" in the cluster head election process. The AMRP of a node u is defined as the mean of the minimum power levels required by all M nodes within the cluster range to reach the node u:

$$AMRP(u) = \frac{\sum_{i=1}^{M} MinPwr(i)}{M} \tag{4.10}$$

During each iteration, a node that is not "covered" by any final cluster head can elect itself to become a new tentative cluster head node based on its probability CH_{prob}. Every node then doubles its CH_{prob} and goes to the next step. Once the node's CH_{prob} reaches 1, the node can become a final cluster head, or it can choose its cluster head as the least cost node from the pool of final cluster head neighbors. If the node completes HEED execution without selecting its final cluster head, then it considers itself uncovered and becomes a final cluster head for the upcoming round.

Once the clusters are formed, all sensors send their data to the cluster head, where the data are aggregated into a single packet. The cluster head nodes form a network backbone, so packets are routed from the cluster head nodes to the sink in a multi-hop fashion over the cluster head nodes.

4.6.2   Simulation Results: All Sensors Active

We compare our CPCP with HEED in scenarios where 400 sensor nodes are deployed either randomly or nonuniformly over a $200 \times 200m^2$ region. In HEED the elected cluster head nodes form a spanning tree for inter-cluster communication in each iteration, and thus we follow this approach for CPCP in these simulations. We assume that each cluster head node aggregates its received data packets into one packet that is sent to the data sink located in the middle of the area.

In HEED, all sensor nodes continue their sensing task after the clusters are formed. Therefore, we adopt the same approach in CPCP for these simulations, and hence all sensor nodes remain in the active state during the Communication Phase of CPCP. In contrast to the previous set of simulations, where the intra-cluster communication was established among a small number of active sensor nodes and their cluster heads, here the cluster head nodes spend a much larger amount of energy in communicating with their cluster members.

70

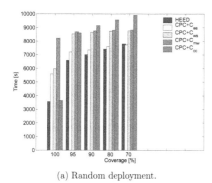

(a) Random deployment.

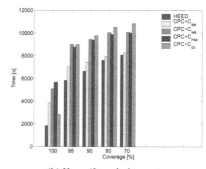

(b) Nonuniform deployment.

Figure 4.12: Comparison of HEED and CPCP in terms of coverage-time.

HEED is a distributed clustering protocol that does not depend on the synchronization of sensor nodes in the network. However, the subsequent broadcasting of announcement messages from the tentative cluster head nodes in each clustering phase requires quite a bit of energy. In CPCP however, the nodes using cost C_{mw} and C_{ws} need to periodically broadcast their remaining energy, which is an additional burden on the limited energy resources. Both clustering algorithms generate uniformly dispersed cluster head nodes. However, in applications where the sensor network has to maintain full coverage, the choice of cluster head nodes significantly impacts the network's coverage-time.

Figure 4.12 shows the network coverage over time for HEED and for CPCP using different cost metrics. As shown in this figure, the results for CPCP from these simulations are quite similar to the results presented in Section 4.5. The minimum-weight cost metric C_{mw} provides 100% coverage for the longest time and the weighted-sum cost metric C_{ws} provides almost full coverage for the longest period of time. The improvement of CPCP over HEED in terms of 100% coverage-time is noticeable using all the cost metrics. Compared with HEED, the time during which the randomly deployed network provides full coverage of the monitored area on average increases by 67% and 125% using C_{ws} and C_{mw}, respectively. In the nonuniformly deployed network this time of full coverage increases even more—by 1.8× and 2.6× using C_{ws} and C_{mw}, respectively, compared with HEED.

HEED gives priority to the nodes with higher remaining energy to be elected as cluster heads. In the case when nodes can manage variable transmission power, the AMRP cost metric (used by the nodes to decide among the best cluster head candidate) depends on the distance between the potential cluster head and its neighboring nodes. However, AMRP

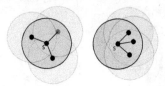

Figure 4.13: Two situations where sensor node S has the same AMRP cost but different coverage redundancy.

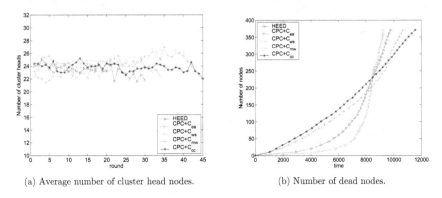

(a) Average number of cluster head nodes.
(b) Number of dead nodes.

Figure 4.14: Comparison of HEED and CPCP in terms of the number of cluster heads per round and the number of dead nodes over time.

does not provide any information about the nodes' spatial distribution and therefore about the redundancy in coverage provided by the nodes. For example, Figure 4.13 shows a node S with three neighboring nodes that are all at the same distance from the node S. In both cases node S had the same AMRP cost since it needs the same transmission power to reach all three neighboring nodes. However, in the first case the sensing area of node S is completely covered by the sensing areas of its neighboring nodes, while in the second case this is not true. Therefore, node S will have higher C_{mw} or C_{ws} costs in the second case. This shows that in coverage-preserving applications the information about the coverage redundancy is crucial to maintaining complete coverage for long periods of time.

Furthermore, CPCP and HEED produce similar numbers of clusters, as illustrated in Figure 4.14a, which shows the number of cluster head nodes during the time in which the network provides up to 90% coverage. The cost for extended coverage-time using coverage-aware cluster head selection is paid by more dead nodes compared to HEED, as shown in

72

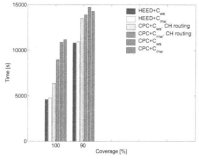

(a) Random deployment of sensor nodes.

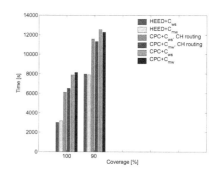

(b) Nonuniform deployment of sensor nodes.

Figure 4.15: Comparison of Hybrid HEED and CPCP in terms of coverage-time for random and nonuniform deployment scenarios.

Figure 4.14b. However, while the network loses fewer nodes using HEED, the network is not able to provide coverage as long as it can using CPCP.

4.6.3 Hybrid HEED: HEED Combined with Coverage-preserving Sensor Activation

Finally, we measure the coverage-time obtained using a hybrid version of HEED. In the *hybrid HEED* protocol, the clusters are formed according to the original HEED algorithm, and this cluster formation stage is followed by the selection of active sensor nodes that are able to maximally cover the network. The C_{ws} and C_{mw} cost metrics are used for the selection of active sensors, while the rest of the nodes are put to sleep. We compare hybrid HEED with two cases of CPCP. The first case corresponds to CPCP described in Section 4.5. The second case corresponds to CPCP where the routing of cluster head packets is done using the cluster head nodes rather than the sensor nodes.

Figure 4.15 shows the lifetime of the network, defined as time for which 100% and 90% network coverage is preserved. Both variants of CPCP significantly outperform the "hybrid HEED" protocol, which again illustrates the importance of making suitable choices for the cluster head nodes for coverage-preserving sensor network applications.

4.7 Which Cost Metric to Use?

In all of our simulations, both coverage-aware cost metrics C_{mw} and C_{ws} outperform the energy-aware cost metric C_{ea} in terms of coverage-time. The minimum-weight C_{mw} cost metric provides the best results (longest coverage-lifetime) in all scenarios where the sensor network has to provide complete (100%) coverage of the monitored area. However, the maintenance of full coverage over the monitored area is extremely expensive, since it requires that non-redundantly covered nodes are always turned on, which shortens their lifetime. The weighted-sum cost metric C_{ws} shows better performance than the minimum-weight cost metric after coverage drops a few percentages, since it provides a more balanced relationship between the node's coverage redundancy and its remaining energy. Therefore, in applications that require the maintenance of full coverage, the minimum-weight cost is the best choice, while for applications that can relax this requirement slightly, the weighted-sum cost is the best choice.

Although the coverage redundancy cost metric C_{cc} depends only on the sensor's coverage, it does not perform well when full coverage is required. This cost metric can potentially be used in small size networks, where data routing is not needed or is done over very small numbers of hops. Finally, C_{ea} performs worse than any other cost metric, and it should not be the choice for any application that requires persistent coverage of the monitored area.

4.8 Summary

In this Chapter we explored different coverage-aware cost metrics for the selection of the cluster head nodes, active nodes and routers in wireless sensor networks whose aim is to maintain coverage of a monitored space. In such coverage-preserving applications, both the remaining energy of the sensor nodes as well as the redundancy in their coverage have to be jointly considered when determining the best candidates for cluster head nodes, active nodes and data routers. Through extensive simulations we illustrated the shortcomings of using remaining energy or coverage redundancy as the only criteria for the decision about the nodes' roles in cluster-based wireless sensor networks. Instead, using the coverage-aware cost metrics prolong coverage-time over the monitored area, by minimizing the use of sensors in sparsely covered areas and those with low remaining energy.

The cost metrics presented in this Chapter can be used for the selection and assignment of different roles to the sensor nodes in a number of the applications. For example, in visual sensor networks these cost metrics can be utilized for the selection of a central camera-node that performs the cluster head role in tracking applications, which collects image data from the other cameras and extracts the most relevant information about the tracking object. Also, the proposed cost metrics can be used for the selection of active camera-nodes over time. Therefore, in the following chapters we will explore further this coverage-aware approach for the camera selection in the visual sensor networks.

Chapter 5

An Overview of Visual Sensor Networks

Camera-based networks have been used for security monitoring and surveillance for a very long time. In these networks, surveillance IP cameras act as independent peers that continuously send video streams to a central processing server, where the video is analyzed by a human operator.

Rapid advances in image sensor technology have enabled the development of cheap (on the order of ten dollars), low-power camera modules in recent years, as evidenced, for example, by the ubiquitous cellular phone cameras. This has given rise to a new research area — visual sensor networks. Visual sensor networks are networks of *wireless camera-nodes*, where the camera-node consists of the imager circuitry, a processor, and a wireless transceiver. In the near future visual sensor networks will provide more suitable solutions, compared with existing networks of high-power and high-resolution cameras, for many image-based applications that assume no infrastructure on site or no time for planning of the cameras' placement.

In visual sensor networks, the camera-nodes can be simply stuck on walls or objects prior to use without the need for preplanning of the cameras' placement, thereby obtaining arbitrary positions/directions. Furthermore, camera-nodes are powered by batteries, and therefore, they do not require a constant power supply. This makes visual sensor networks suitable for use in applications where temporary monitoring is needed and in applications that require fast deployment and removal of the camera network. All these characteristics, together with a flexible topology, the ability to scale to hundreds of image sensor nodes, the absence of long cables for camera networking, and the broad spectrum of applications are some of the many reasons that visual sensor networks are more attractive than traditional surveillance networking systems.

5.1 Characteristics of Image Sensors

Image sensors posses several characteristics that make them unique. In particular, their distinctive characteristics compared to other sensor types are:

- **Image sensor**

  Image sensors are composed of a large number of photosensitive cell arrays, which measure the light intensity from different sources determined by an optical lens. One measurement of the image sensor provides a two dimensional set of data points, which we see as an image. The additional dimensionality of the data compared with other sensor types results in higher complexity in data analysis and a higher cost for data processing and transmission.

- **Sensing model**

  A camera's sensing model is inherently different from the sensing model of any other type of sensor. Typically, it is assumed that a sensor node can collect data from its vicinity, as determined by the node's sensing range, which is often approximated by a circular sensing area around the node. A camera is characterized by a *directional sensing model* — it captures the images of distant objects from a certain direction. Also, a camera is characterized by its *depth of field*, which is defined as the distance between the closest and the furthest object that the camera can capture sharply. Therefore, the two-dimensional sensing range of traditional sensor nodes is, in the case of the cameras, replaced by the 3-dimensional viewing volume (called the viewing frustum).

5.2 Introduction to Multiple-view Geometry

Extraction of relevant visual information is based on multiple-view vision concepts. In this Section, we provide a brief overview of the perspective camera model and the most important image processing techniques for scene reconstruction.

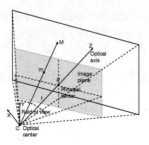

Figure 5.1: The pinhole camera model.

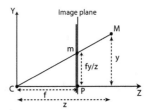

Figure 5.2: Projection of point M(x,y,z) in the image plane.

5.2.1 Pinhole Camera Model

The pinhole camera, shown in Figure 5.1, is an ideal model of a camera used for geometric representation of imaging. The image plane is located at a distance f (focal length) from the optical center C of the camera. The line from the camera's center normal to the image plane is called the optical axis of the camera. A 3D point is projected onto the image plane with a line containing this point and the optical center. Four planes, starting from the camera's optical center, form the visible volume of the camera, also known as its viewing frustum. The angle between two inclined planes is known as the angle of view or field of view (FoV).

The relationship between the 3D coordinates of a scene point and the coordinates of its projection onto the camera's image plane are given by *the perspective projection model*. From Figure 5.2, a 3D point M $(x, y, z)^T$ is mapped to the point $(fx/z, fy/z, f)^T$ on the image plane. When the 3D point and its projection on the image plane are given in homogeneous coordinates [65], the perspective projection can be expressed in matrix form as:

$$\begin{pmatrix} fx \\ fy \\ z \end{pmatrix} = \begin{bmatrix} f & 0 & 0 & 0 \\ 0 & f & 0 & 0 \\ 0 & 0 & 1 & 0 \end{bmatrix} \begin{pmatrix} x \\ y \\ z \\ 1 \end{pmatrix}$$

or:

$$z\mathbf{m} = P\mathbf{M}$$

The matrix that describes the linear mapping is called the camera projection matrix P, and $\mathbf{M} = (x, y, z, 1)^T$ and $\mathbf{m} = (fx/z, fy/z, f)^T$ are the homogeneous coordinates of a 3D point and its projection on the image plane. The full rank 3x4 projection matrix P can be factored as:

$$P = K \begin{bmatrix} R & | & \mathbf{t} \end{bmatrix}$$

where K represents the *camera calibration matrix*, R is the rotation matrix and $\mathbf{t}$ is a translation vector. The calibration matrix contains the camera's *intrinsic* parameters (focal distance f, center of image plane (o_x, o_y), pixel sizes s_x and s_y) needed for transformation from camera coordinates to pixel coordinates. The position and orientation of the camera is described by *extrinsic* parameters, stored in the rotation matrix R and the translation vector $\mathbf{t}$.

The projection of a point in space to the image plane can be modelled as the ray passing through the camera's optical center and this point in space. This optical ray that passes through the point $\mathbf{m} = (u, v, 1)$ is the locus of all points in space that project onto $\mathbf{m}$. This is described by the projection equation:

$$\zeta\mathbf{m} = P\mathbf{M}$$

where ζ represents depth or distance of $\mathbf{M}$ from the focal plane of the camera, and it contains an arbitrary scale factor.

5.2.2   Epipolar Geometry

The two-view of epipolar geometry presents the geometry of two perspective views of the same 3D scene. When there is no occlusion, most of the scene points $\mathbf{M} = (x, y, z, 1)^T$ can be simultaneously seen from both views. The point $\mathbf{M} = (x, y, z, 1)^T$ is projected to the left and right view as $\mathbf{m_l} = (u_l, v_l, 1)$ and $\mathbf{m_r} = (u_r, v_r, 1)$, which are called corresponding

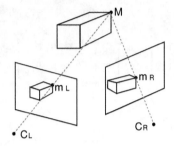

Figure 5.3: Epipolar geometry.

points, and their relationship is given by the epipolar geometry. Detailed information about epipolar geometry can be found in [66]. The correspondence between the images is crucial for scene reconstruction. The precision of scene reconstruction depends on the accuracy of the corresponding points, as well as on the accuracy of the knowledge about the camera setup and the scene itself.

5.3   Characteristics of Visual Sensor Networks

The problems and related research challenges of visual sensor networks go beyond those of existing wireless sensor networks. Some of the main characteristics and requirements of visual sensor networks are listed next.

- Resource Requirements

  The lifetime of battery-operated camera-motes is limited by the energy consumption, which is proportional to their energy required for data processing and data transmission over the wireless medium. Given the large amount of data generated by the camera-motes, both processing and transmitting image data are quite costly in terms of energy, much more so than for other types of sensor networks. Furthermore, visual sensor networks require large bandwidth for transmitting image data. Thus both energy and bandwidth are even more constrained than in other types of wireless sensor networks.

- Local Processing

  Local (on-board) processing of the image data reduces the total amount of data that needs to be communicated through the network. Local processing can involve simple image processing algorithms (such as background substraction for motion/object detection, edge detection) as well as more complex image/vision processing algorithms (such as feature extraction, object classification, scene reasoning). Thus, depending on the application, the camera-nodes may require different levels of intelligence, as determined by the complexity of the processing algorithms they use [67]. For example, low-level processing algorithms (such as frame differencing for motion detection or edge detection algorithms) can provide a camera-node with more information about the current environment, and help it decide whether it is necessary to transmit the captured image or whether it should continue processing the image at a higher level. More complex vision algorithms (such as objects feature extraction, object classification, etc.) enable cameras to reason about the captured phenomena, such as to provide basic classification of the captured object. Furthermore, the cameras can collaborate by exchanging the detected object features, enabling further processing to collectively reason about the object's appearance or behavior. At this point the visual sensor network becomes a user-independent, intelligent system of distributed cameras that provides only relevant information about the monitored phenomena. Therefore, the increased complexity of vision processing algorithms results in highly intelligent camera systems that are oftentimes called smart camera networks [68].

- Real-time Performance

  Most applications of visual sensor networks require real-time data from the camera-nodes, which imposes strict boundaries on maximum allowable delays of data from the sources (cameras) to the user (sink). The real-time performance of a visual sensor network is affected by the time required for image data processing and for the transmission of the processed data throughout the network.

  The amount of on-board processing affects the real-time performances of a camera network. An embedded processor at the camera-node dictates the processing speed. Constrained by limited energy resources as well as by allowable delays, most camera-nodes have processors that support only lightweight processing algorithms.

  On the network side, the maximum data rate is limited by the channel bandwidth, which is determined by the wireless networking standard employed. However, the maximum physical data rate cannot be realized in most networks. The existing contention-based MAC protocols that provide access to the shared wireless channel do not completely solve the packet collision problem, which is the main reason for increased data delays. On the other hand, TDMA-based MAC protocols successfully cope with collision problem, but they require tight synchronization and do not have the situation-aware flexibility for transmitting data. Furthermore, upon detection of an event, the camera-nodes can suddenly inject large amounts of data in the network, which can cause data congestion and increase data delays.

Different error protection schemes can affect the real-time transmission of image data through the network as well. Commonly used error protection schemes, such as automated-repeat-request (ARQ) and forward-error-correction (FEC) have been investigated in order to increase the reliability of wireless data transmissions [69]. However, due to the tight delay constraints, methods such as ARQ are not suitable to be used in visual sensor networks. On the other hand, FEC schemes usually require long blocks in order to perform well, which again can jeopardize delay constraints.

Finally, multi-hop routing is the preferred routing method in wireless sensor networks due to its energy-efficiency. However, multi-hop routing may result in increased delays, due to queueing and data processing at the intermediate nodes. Thus, the total delay from the data source (camera-node) to the sink increases with the number of hops on the routing path.

- Precise Location and Orientation Information

  In wireless sensor networks, information about the location of the sensor nodes is crucial for many routing and sensor management protocols. In visual sensor networks, most of the image processing algorithms require information about the locations of the camera-nodes as well as information about the cameras' orientations. This information can be obtained through a camera calibration process, which retrieves information on the cameras' intrinsic and extrinsic parameters. The extrinsic parameters describe the camera's placement in a world reference coordinate system, given by a rotation matrix and translation vector. The intrinsic parameters are related to the camera circuitry, and determine the focal length, the position of the principal point (center of the camera's image plane) and skew [66]. Estimation of calibration parameters usually requires knowledge of a set of feature point correspondences among the images of the cameras. When this is not provided, the cameras can be calibrated up to a similarity transformation [66], meaning that only relative coordinates and orientations of the cameras with the respect to each other can be determined.

- Synchronization

  The information content of an image may become meaningless without proper information about the time at which this image was captured. Many processing tasks that involve multiple cameras (such as object localization) depend on highly synchronized cameras' snapshots. Synchronization protocols developed for wireless sensor networks [70] can be successfully used for synchronization of visual sensor networks as well.

- Data Storage

  The cameras generate large amounts of data over time, which in some cases should be stored for later analysis. An example is monitoring of remote areas by a group of camera-nodes, where the frequent transmissions of captured image data to a remote sink would quickly exhaust the cameras' energy resources. Thus, in these cases the camera-nodes should be equipped with memories of larger capacity in order to store the data. To minimize the amount of data that requires storage, the camera-nodes should classify the data according to its importance by using spatio-temporal analysis of image frames, and decide which data should have priority to be stored. For example, if an application is interested in information about some particular object, then the background can be highly compressed and stored, or even completely discarded.

  The stored image data usually becomes less important over time, so it can be substituted with newly acquired data. In addition, reduction of redundancy in the data collected by cameras with overlapped views can be achieved via local communication and processing. This enables the cameras to reduce their needs for storage space by keeping only data of unique image regions. Finally, by increasing the available memory, more complex processing tasks can be supported on-board, which in return can reduce data transmissions and reduce the space needed for storage of processed data.

- Autonomous Camera Collaboration

  Visual sensor networks are envisioned as distributed and autonomous systems, where cameras collaborate and, based on exchanged information, reason autonomously about the captured event and decide how to proceed. Through collaboration, the cameras relate the events captured in the images and they enhance their understanding of the environment. Similar to wireless sensor networks, visual sensor networks should be data-centric, where captured events are described by their names and attributes.

Communication between cameras should be based on the uniform ontology for the description of the event and interpretation of the scene dynamics [71].

- Camera Management

  An important issue in visual sensor networks is the problem of scheduling the activity of the camera-nodes, so that they provide the application with sufficient information, while the network's resources are utilized efficiently. This problem is inherited from traditional wireless sensor networks, but solutions must be adapted to the unique aforementioned characteristics of visual sensor networks and the fact that the visual sensor network needs to cover a 3-dimensional space.

5.4 Applications of Visual Sensor Networks

Visual Sensor Networks can be used in many applications. We list some of the most popular applications here:

- Surveillance — Surveillance has been the primary application of camera-based networks for a long time, where the monitoring of large public areas (such as airports, subways, etc.) is performed by hundreds or even thousands of IP-based security cameras. However, these networks of cameras usually assume the existence of specific infrastructure at the deployment site. Since cameras usually provide raw video streams, acquiring important information from collected image data requires a huge amount of processing and human resources, making it time-consuming and prone to error. Current efforts in visual sensor networking are concentrated toward advancing the existing surveillance technology by utilizing intelligent methods for extracting information from image data locally on the camera-mote, thereby reducing the amount of data traffic. At the same time, visual sensor networks integrate resource-aware camera management policies and wireless networking aspects with surveillance-specific tasks. Thus, visual sensor networks can be seen as a next generation of surveillance systems that are not limited by the absence of infrastructure, nor do they require large processing resources at one central server. These networks are adaptable to the environment dynamics, autonomous, and able to respond timely to a user's requests by providing an immediate view from any desired viewpoint or by analyzing and providing information from specific, user determined areas.

- Environmental monitoring — Visual sensor networks can be used for monitoring remote and inaccessible areas over a long period of time. In these applications, energy-efficient operations are particularly important in order to prolong monitoring over an extended period of time. Oftentimes the cameras are combined with other types of sensors into a heterogeneous network, such that the cameras are triggered only when an event is detected by other sensors used in the network [72].

- Smart homes — There are situations (such as patients in hospitals or people with disabilities), where a person must be under the constant care of others. Visual sensor networks can provide continuous monitoring of people, and using smart algorithms the network can provide information about the person needing care, such as information about any unusual behavior or an emergency situation.

- Smart meeting rooms — Remote participants in a meeting can enjoy a dynamic visual experience using visual sensor network technology.

- Tele-presence systems — Tele-presence systems enable a remote user to "visit" some location that is monitored by a collection of cameras. For example, museums, galleries or exhibition rooms can be covered by a network of camera-nodes that provide live video streams to a user who wishes to access the place remotely (e.g., over the Internet). The system is able to provide the user with any current view from any viewing point, and thus it provides the sense of being physically present at a remote location through interaction with the system's interface [73]. Tele-reality aims to synthesize realistic novel views from images acquired from multiple cameras [74].

5.5 Research Directions in Visual Sensor Networks

Since visual sensor networks have started to gain popularity only over the last decade, research in this area is still in its infancy. Visual sensor networks are based on several diverse research fields, including image/vision processing, communication and networking, and distributed and embedded system processing architectures. Thus, the design complexity involves finding the best trade-off between performance and different aspects of these networks. These aspects are defined through a set of operational parameters, which reflect different technologies used in the design of a visual network and can be adjusted for the particular application. According to Hengstler and Aghajan [75] the design of a camera-based network involves mapping application requirements to a set of network operation parameters that are

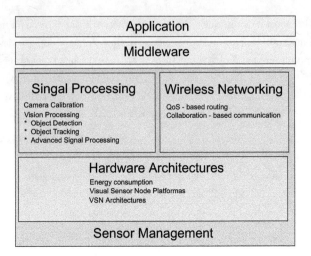

| Application |
| Middleware |

Singal Processing	**Wireless Networking**
Camera Calibration Vision Processing * Object Detection * Object Tracking * Advanced Signal Processing	QoS - based routing Collaboration - based communication

Hardware Architectures

Energy consumption
Visual Sensor Node Platformas
VSN Architectures

Sensor Management

Figure 5.4: Several research areas that contribute to the development of visual sensor networks.

generally related to the field of network topology, sensing, processing, communication and resources.

Due to its interdisciplinary nature, the research directions in visual sensor networks are numerous and diverse. In the following sections we present an overview of the ongoing research in several areas vital to visual sensor networks: vision processing, wireless networking, camera-node hardware architectures, sensor management, and middleware, as illustrated in Figure 5.4.

5.6 Camera Calibration and Localization

In visual sensor networks precise information about the cameras' locations and orientations is crucial for many vision processing algorithms. This information is obtained through the camera calibration process, which refers to the process of estimating the camera's orientation matrix R and its location $-RT$ (T is the translation vector) based on points that the camera sees and that belong to a set of feature points.

The calibration of cameras can be done in a centralized manner, by sending the images from all cameras to one processing center. However, this method is expensive in terms of bandwidth and energy due to the required transmission of large amounts of data. Therefore,

86

distributed and energy-efficient algorithms for camera calibration are required in resource-constrained visual sensor networks.

Due to the ad-hoc deployment of camera-motes and the absence of human support after deployment, the calibration algorithms for visual sensor networks should be autonomous. Since usually there is no prior information about the network's vision graph (a graph which provides information about overlapped cameras' FoVs), or about the environment, finding correspondences across cameras (presented as a set of points in one camera's image plane that correspond to the points in another camera's image) is complicated and error prone. Ideally, cameras should have the ability to self-calibrate based on their observations from the environment. The first step in this process involves finding sets of cameras that image the same scene points. Having cameras farther apart from each other makes the problem of matching correspondences among images even more challenging. Finding correspondences among these cameras may require excessive, energy expensive inter-camera communication, which has to be reduced. On the other hand, limited transmission ranges of the camera-motes can limit communication between them. Therefore, camera calibration in a visual sensor network is challenged by finding the cameras' precise extrinsic parameters based on existing calibration procedures taken from computer vision, but considering the communication constraints and energy limitations of camera-motes. These calibration methods should cope successfully with changes in the communication graph (caused by variable channel conditions) and changes in the visual graph (due to the loss of cameras or a change in the cameras' positions and orientations).

Calibration based on a known object is a common calibration method from computer vision that is widely adopted in visual sensor networks [76, 77]. In [76] Barton-Sweeney et al. present a light-wight protocol for camera calibration based on such an approach, where the network contains a fraction of wireless nodes equipped with CMOS camera modules, while the rest of the nodes us unique modulated LED emissions in order to uniquely identify themselves to the cameras. This calibration method requires distance information among the cameras, which is obtained through finding epipoles among the pairs of cameras. In the specific case when a common target (node) is observed by two cameras that can also see each other, the distances between the cameras and the node can be determined up to a scale factor [78]. However, in the more common case when a pair of cameras cannot observe each other but they can still observe a common part of the scene, the authors estimate the fundamental matrix (based on a minimum of 8 points in the common view) that is then used for estimating the cameras' epipoles. This method for estimating cameras' epipoles results in noisy data, indicating the need for knowledge of the distances between the observed nodes, which enables constrained optimization of the epipoles estimation problem. Thus, in [76] the authors do not provide fully automatic camera calibration methods, but instead they point out the difficulty of finding appropriate network configurations that can ease the calibration process.

Funiak et al. [77] provide a distributed method for camera calibration based on collaborative tracking of a moving target by multiple cameras. Here, the simultaneous localization and tracking (SLAT) problem is analyzed, which refers to estimation of both the trajectory of the object and the poses of the cameras. The proposed solution to the SLAT problem is based on an approximation of a Kalman filter. The restricting networking conditions are not considered in the proposed method.

Devarajan et al. [79] present a distributed algorithm for camera calibration, which is performed on a vision graph formed by drawing the edges between the cameras that observe the same scene points from different perspectives. As a result of calibration, each camera estimates its local parameters (location, orientation and focal length), parameters for each of its neighbors in the vision graph, and 3D positions of the scene points that correspond to the matched image features. The cameras that share a sufficient number of scene points form clusters and perform local calibration – estimation of camera parameters and unknown scene points based on 2D image correspondences. For local calibration purposes, each cluster needs to have a minimum of three cameras, and they all need to observe at least 8 corresponding points. After the initial estimation, the local calibration results are refined using a nonlinear minimization method called bundle adjustment, which minimizes the Mahalanobis distance between the real and estimated 2D correspondences (obtained based on the estimated cameras' parameters) over each cluster of cameras. Finally, to ensure that correspondences between the camera parameter estimates are accurate, the authors remove outliers using a RANSAC-type algorithm. The performance of the calibration algorithm is evaluated through simulation and using real data sets. The results of simulations show the advantages of using the distributed method over centralized calibration, since the average error in the estimated parameters is similar in both cases, but the distributed estimation requires less time since it performs the optimization over a smaller number of estimating parameters.

It is notable that most of the algorithms for camera calibration in visual sensor networks are based on existing calibration methods established in computer vision, and rarely are they influenced by the underlying network. Thus, future camera calibration algorithms should explore how these algorithms are constrained from the networking side. Methods for multi-camera calibration should consider requirements for reliable and energy-efficient inter-camera communication. Also, the calibration methods should be robust to the network's dynamics: for example, considering how the addition of new cameras or the loss of existing cameras affect the calibration process. Above all, the calibration algorithms should be light-weight, meaning that they should not be based on extensive processing operations. Instead, they should be easily implementable on the hardware platforms of existing camera-motes. Due to the ad-hoc nature of visual sensor networks, future research is required to develop camera calibration algorithms that determine precise calibration parameters using a fully automatic approach that requires minimal or no a-priori knowledge of network distances, network geometry or corresponding feature points.

5.7 Vision-based Signal Processing

The appearance of small CMOS image sensors and the development of distributed wireless sensor networks opens a door to a new era in embedded vision processing. The challenge is how to adapt existing vision processing algorithms to be used in resource-constrained distributed networks of mostly low-resolution cameras. The first and the main constraint comes from the amount of data that can be transmitted through the network. While wireless sensor networks are designed and optimized for transmission of small amounts of data in mind, in visual sensor networks this is not the case. Additionally, most vision processing algorithms are developed without regard to any processing limitations. Furthermore, timing constraints of existing algorithms need to be carefully reconsidered, as the data may travel over multiple hops. Finally, many vision processing algorithms are developed for single camera systems, so these algorithms now need to be adapted for multi-camera distributed systems.

The limited processing capabilities of camera-motes dictate a need for light-weight vision processing algorithms in visual sensor networks. However, distributed processing of image data and data fusion from multiple image sources requires more intelligent embedded vision algorithms. As the processing algorithms start to become more demanding (such as those that rely on extraction of feature points and feature matching across multiple cameras' views) the processing capabilities can become a bottleneck. Considering the hierarchical model for vision processing provided in [75], here we describe the main vision processing tasks for visual sensor networks.

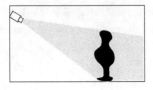

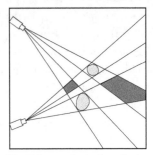

(a) Two cameras observe a person from different positions. The cameras' cones are swept around the person's silhouette.

(b) Polygons obtained as the intersection of planar projections of cones in the case of two objects. Visual hull presents the largest volume in which an object can reside. The dark-colored polygons do not contain any objects.

Figure 5.5: Finding the polygons that contain people based on a projection of the person' silhouettes on the planar scene [1].

5.7.1 Occlusion Handling and Occupancy Reasoning

The initial phase of visual data processing usually involves object detection. Object detection may trigger a camera's processing activity and data communication. Object detection is mostly based on light-weight background substraction algorithms and presents the first step toward collective reasoning by the camera-motes about the objects that occupy the monitored space. In light-weight algorithms for scene analysis the interest is not on the object's individual features but more on simple information about the presence and quantity of objects in the monitored scene.

Many applications of visual sensor networks require reasoning about the presence of objects in the scene. In occupancy reasoning, the visual sensor network is not interested in extracting an individual object's features, but instead extracting the state of the scene based on light-weight image processing algorithms. An example of such occupancy reasoning in visual sensor networks is the estimation of the number of people in a crowded scene, as discussed in [1]. Here the estimates are obtained using a planar projection of the scene's visual hull, as illustrated in Figure 5.5. Since the objects may be occluded, the exact number of objects cannot be determined, but instead lower and upper bounds on the number of objects in each polygon are tracked. The estimated bounds on the number of objects are updated over time using a history tree, so that the lower and upper bounds converge toward the exact number of objects in each polygon.

Determining good camera-network deployments and the number of camera-motes to use is also addressed in recent work. For example, in [80] Yang et al. study a model for managing (tasking) a set of cameras that collectively reason about the occupancy of the monitored area. Their goal is to provide an upper bound on the number of cameras needed to reason about the occupancy for a given accuracy. This task is performed by minimizing the area potentially occupied by the moving objects. Using the Monte-Carlo method, the authors in [80] find the number of cameras necessary to provide a visual hull area for one object. However, in the case of multiple objects in the scene, the visual hull area does not converge to the actual area covered by the objects, due to occlusions. Thus, the authors compare several heuristic approaches (uniform, greedy, clustering, optimal) for finding a subset of the cameras that minimize the visual hull area for the scenario with multiple objects in the scene.

Since detection of objects on the scene is usually the first step in image analysis, it is important to minimize the chances of objects' fault detection. Thus, reliability and light-weight operations will continue to be the main concerns of image processing algorithms for object detection and occupancy reasoning.

5.7.2 Object Tracking

Object tracking is a common task for many applications of visual sensor networks. Object tracking is a challenging task since it is computationally intensive and it requires real-time data processing. The basic methods for target tracking include temporal differencing and template correlation matching [81]. Temporal differencing requires finding the regions in frames separated in time that have been changed, and thus it fails if the object stops moving or if it gets occluded. On the other hand, template correlation matching aims to find the region of an image that best correlates to an image template. This method is not robust to changes in the object's appearance, such as object size, orientation or even light conditions. Sophisticated tracking algorithms, which rely on motion parameter estimation and probability estimates (such as tracking algorithms based on Kalman filtering [82] or particle filtering [83]) are suitable for smart camera networks with advanced processing capabilities.

The availability of multiple views in visual sensor networks improves tracking reliability, but with the price of an increased communication overhead among the cameras. Therefore, in resource-constrained visual sensor networks it is important to use lightweight processing algorithms and to minimize the data load that has to be communicated among the cameras. Lau et al. [84] provide an example of a simple algorithm for tracking multiple targets based on hue histograms. After background substraction and segmentation, the histogram of detected blobs in the scene is found and then compared with the histograms found for previous frames in order to track the objects.

Ko and Berry [85] investigate a distributed scheme for target tracking in a multi-camera environment. Their collaborative strategy is based on establishing information links between the cameras that detect the target (initiators) and their neighboring cameras that can share information about the tracked target. The cameras extract several target features (edge histogram, UV color histogram, local position of target) which are correlated across the nodes in order to decide whether information links should be established between the nodes. Such an approach improves the accuracy of the target detection and significantly reduces the communication load.

The success of the proposed tracking algorithms can be jeopardized in the case when the tracked objects are occluded. Object occlusion, which happens when a camera looses sight of an object due to obstruction by another object, is an unavoidable problem in visual sensor networks. Although in most cases the positions of moving occluders cannot be predicted, still it is expected that a multi-camera system can handle the occlusion problem more easily due to providing multiple object views. This problem is discussed in [86], where the authors examine the dependance of single object tracking on prior information about the movement of the tracked object and about static occluders. The real challenge in visual sensor networks however, is to avoid losing the tracked object due to occlusions in the situation when not all cameras are available for tracking at the same time. Thus, future research should be directed toward examining the best sensor management policies for selecting camera-motes that will enable multiple target views, thereby reducing the chances of occlusion while using the minimum number of cameras.

5.7.3   Advanced Signal Processing in VSNs

Many novel applications of visual sensor networks are based on advanced vision processing that provides a thorough analysis of the objects' appearances and behaviors, thereby providing a better understanding of the relationships among the objects and situation awareness to the user. For example, a visual sensor network can be used not only to track human movements, but also to interpret these movements in order to recognize semantically meaningful gestures. Human gesture analysis and behavior recognition have gained increasing interest in the research community and are used in a number of applications such as surveillance, video conferencing, smart homes and assisted living. Behavior analysis applications require collaboration among the cameras, which exchange pre-processed, high level descriptions of the observed scene, rather than the raw image information. In order to reduce the amount of information exchanged between the cameras, research is directed toward finding an effective way of describing the scene and providing the semantic meaning of the extracted data (features). An example of such research is provided in [87], where Teixeira et al. describe a camera-based network that provides symbolic information in order to summarize the motion activity of people. The extracted basic functions of human activity are analyzed using a sensing grammar, which provides the probability likelihood of each outcome. This hierarchical inference model is used to reason about the macroscopic behaviors of people – the behavior in some area over a long period of time.

Human behavior interpretation and gesture analysis often use explicit shape models that provide a priori knowledge of the human body in 3D. Oftentimes, these models assume a certain type of body movement, which eases the gesture interpretation problem in the case of body self-occlusion. Recent work of Aghajan et al. [88] provides a framework for human behavior interpretation based on a 3-D human model for estimation of a user's posture from multiple cameras' views. This model is reconstructed from previous model instances and current multiple camera views, and it contains information on geometric body configuration, color/texture of body parts and motion information. After fitting ellipses to corresponding body parts (segments), human posture is estimated by minimizing the distance between the posture and the ellipses.

Another approach in designing context-aware visual based networks involves using multimodal information for the analysis and interpretation of the objects' dynamics. In addition to low-power camera-motes, such systems may contain other types of sensors such as audio, vibration, thermal and PIR. By fusing multimodal information from various nodes, such a network can provide better models for understanding an object's behavior and group interactions.

The aforementioned vision processing tasks require extracting features about an event, which in the case of energy and memory constrained camera-motes can be hard or even impossible to achieve, especially in real-time. Thus, although it is desirable to have high-resolution data features, costly feature extractions actually should be limited. This implies the need for finding optimal ways to determine when feature extraction tasks can be performed and when they should be skipped or left to other active cameras, without degrading overall performance. Also, most of the current work still use a centralized approach for data acquisition and fusion. Thus, future research should be directed toward migrating the process of decision making to the sensors, and toward dynamically finding the best camera-mote that can serve as a fusion center to combine extracted information from all active camera-motes.

5.8   Sensor Management

In redundantly deployed visual sensor networks a subset of cameras can perform continuous monitoring and provide information with a desired quality. This subset of active cameras can be changed over time, which enables balancing of the cameras' energy consumption, while spreading the monitoring task among the cameras. In such a scenario the decision about the camera-motes' activity and scheduling (determining the duration of their activity) is based on sensor management policies. Sensor management policies define the selection and scheduling of the camera-motes' activity in such a way that the visual information from selected cameras satisfies the application-specified requirements while the use of camera resources is minimized. Various quality metrics are used in the evaluation of sensor management policies, such as the energy-efficiency of the selection method or the quality of the gathered image data from the selected cameras. In addition, camera management policies are directed by the application: for example, target tracking usually requires selection of cameras that cover only a part of the scene that contains the non-occluded object, while monitoring of large areas requires the selection of cameras with the largest combined FoV.

While energy-efficient organization of camera-motes is oftentimes addressed by camera management policies, the quality of the data produced by the network is the main concern of the application. Table 5.1 compares several camera management policies considering energy efficiency and bandwidth allocation as two quality metrics for camera selection in two common applications – target tracking and monitoring of large scenes.

Monitoring of large areas (such as parking lots, public areas, large stores, etc.) requires complete coverage of the area at every point in time. Such an application is analyzed in [89], where Dagher et al. provide an optimal strategy for allocating parts of the monitored region

Sensor management policy	QOS CRITERIA		APPLICATION		GOAL OF SENSOR MANAGEMENT METRIC
	Energy efficiency	Bandwidth allocation	Scene monitoring	Object tracking	
Dagher et al. [89]	Yes	No	Yes	No	Battery lifetime optimization
Park et al. [90]	No	No	Yes	No	Quality of view for every 3D point
Soro et al. [91]	Yes	No	Yes	No	Exploring trade-offs between the image quality of reconstructed views and energy efficiency
Zamora et al. [92]	Yes	No	No	Yes	Coordinated-wake up policies for energy conservation
Yang et al. [93]	No	Yes	No	Yes	Proposed several sensor selection policies (random, event-based, view-based, priority-based) that consider bandwidth constraints
Pahalawatta et al. [82]	Yes	No	No	Yes	Maximize sum of information utility provided by the active sensors subjected to the average energy that can be used by the network
Ercan et al. [86]	No	No	No	Yes	Object occlusions avoidance

Table 5.1: Comparison of visual sensor management policies.

to the cameras while maximizing the battery lifetime of the camera-motes. The optimal fractions of regions covered by every camera are found in a centralized way at the base station. The cameras use JPEG2000 to encode the allocated region such that the cost per bit transmission is reduced according to the fraction received from the base station. However, this sensor management policy only considers the coverage of a 2D plane, without occlusions and perspective effects, which makes it harder to use in a real situation.

Oftentimes the quality of a reconstructed view from a set of selected cameras is used as a criterion for the evaluation of camera selection policies. Park et al. [90] use distributed look-up tables to rank the cameras according to how well they image a specific location, and based on this they choose the best candidates that provide images of the desired location. Their selection criterion is based on the fact that the error in the captured image increases as the object gets further away from the center of the viewing frustum. Thus, they divide the frustum of each camera into smaller unit volumes (subfrustums). Then, based on the Euclidian distance of each 3D point to the centers of subfrustums that contain this 3D point, they sort the cameras and find the most favorable camera that contains this point in its field of view. The look-up table entries for each 3D location are propagated through the network in order to build a sorted list of favorable cameras. Thus, camera selection is based exclusively on the quality of the image data provided by the selected cameras, while the resource constraints are not considered.

A similar problem of finding the the best camera candidates is investigated in [91]. In this work, we propose several cost metrics for the selection of a set of camera-motes that provide images used for reconstructing a view from a user-specified view point. Two types of metrics are considered: coverage-aware cost metrics and quality-aware cost metrics. The coverage-aware cost metrics consider the remaining energy of the camera-motes and the coverage of the indoor space, and favor the selection of the cameras with higher remaining energy and more redundant coverage. The quality-aware cost metrics favor the selection of the cameras that provide images from a similar view point as the user's view point. Thus, these camera selection methods provide a trade-off between network lifetime and the quality of the reconstructed images.

In order to reduce the energy consumption of cameras Zamora et al. [92] explore distributed power management of camera-motes based on coordinated node wake-ups. The proposed policy assumes that each camera-mote is awake for a certain period of time, after which the camera-mote decides whether it should enter the low-power state based on the timeout statuses of its neighboring nodes. Alternatively, camera-motes can decide whether to enter the low-power state based on voting from other neighboring cameras.

Selection of the best cameras for target tracking has been discussed often [82, 86]. In [82] Pahalawatta et al. present a camera selection method for target tracking applications used in energy-constrained visual sensor networks. The camera nodes are selected by minimizing an information utility function (obtained as the uncertainty of the estimated posterior distribution of a target) subject to energy constraints. However, the information obtained from the selected cameras can be lost in the case of object occlusions. This occlusion problem is further discussed in [86], where Ercan et al. propose a method for camera selection in the case when the tracked object becomes occluded by static or moving occluders. Finding the best camera set for object tracking involves minimizing the MSE of the object position's estimates. Such a greedy heuristic for camera selection shows results close to optimal and outperforms naive heuristics, such as selection of the closest set of cameras to the target, or uniformly spaced cameras. The authors here assume that some information about the scene is known in advance, such as the positions of static occluders, and the object and dynamic occluders' prior probabilities for location estimates.

Although a large volume of data is transmitted in visual sensor networks, none of the aforementioned works consider channel bandwidth utilization. This problem is investigated in [93] where Yang et al. provide a bandwidth management framework which, based on different camera selection policies and video content, dynamically coordinates the bandwidth requirements among the selected cameras' flows. The bandwidth estimation is provided at the MAC layer of each camera-node, and this information is sent to a centralized bandwidth coordinator that allocates the bandwidth to the selected cameras. The centralized bandwidth allocator guarantees that each camera has the minimum bandwidth available, but the flexibility of distributed bandwidth allocation is lost.

In visual sensor networks, sensor management policies are needed to assure balance between the oftentimes opposite requirements imposed by the wireless networking and vision processing tasks. While reducing energy consumption by limiting data transmissions is the primary challenge of energy-constrained visual sensor networks, the quality of the image data and application QoS improve as the network provides more data. In such an environment, the optimization methods for sensor management developed for wireless sensor networks are oftentimes hard to directly apply to visual sensor networks. Such sensor management policies usually do not consider the event-driven nature of visual sensor networks, nor do they consider the unpredictability of data traffic caused by an event detection.

Thus, more research is needed to further explore sensor management for visual sensor networks. Since sensor management policies depend on the underlying networking policies and vision processing, future research lies in the intersection of finding the best trade-offs between these two aspects of visual sensor networks. Additional work is needed to compare the performance of different camera-mote scheduling sensor policies, including asynchronous (where every camera follows its own on-off schedule) and synchronous (where cameras are divided into different sets, so that in each moment one set of cameras is active) policies. From an application perspective, it would be interesting to explore sensor management policies for supporting multiple applications utilizing a single visual sensor network.

5.9   Communication Protocols

In visual sensor networks the characteristics of the image data and vision perception strongly influence the communication protocols and data transmission in the network. Thus, existing communication protocols developed for "traditional" wireless sensor networks cannot simply be applied to visual sensor networks. For example, in [2] we analyzed the performance of a coverage-aware routing protocol that was initially developed for wireless sensor networks, when this protocol is applied to a network of camera-motes. Although both types of networks are constrained with the same energy resource limitations and with the same application QoS requirements (in terms of full area coverage), there is no simple mapping of routing strategies from one type of network to the other. In visual sensor networks, spatially distant cameras can still observe a common scene (illustrated in Figure 5.6), which is the reason why this coverage-based routing scheme did not perform in the same way as in the case when it is used in a wireless sensor network. This example shows that any communication model for visual sensor networks has to include the visual acquisition model of cameras, in order to provide the most suitable strategies for collaborative data communication.

Existing communication protocols for wireless sensor networks are mostly focused on the energy-efficiency aspects of data communication, thereby neglecting the specific needs for high-rate data and low-delay requirements of visual sensor networks. Therefore, the main question remains: (how) can we adapt existing communication protocols developed for "traditional" wireless sensor networks for use in visual sensor networks? Or, are entirely new communication protocols needed to support data transmission in VSNs?

The main difference between the communication models of "traditional" and visual sensor networks is caused by the amount of data produced in both types of networks. In contrast to "traditional" sensor networks, visual sensor networks are usually event-driven networks,

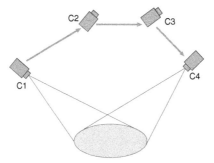

Figure 5.6: Cameras C1 and C4 observe the same part of the scene, but are not in communication range of each other. Thus, data routing is performed over other camera-motes [2].

where captured events trigger the injection of large amounts of data into the network from multiple sources. The actual amount of data sent by each camera-mote depends on the processing algorithm used (for example, the camera-mote may send only information about extracted edges, segments, or the whole image), which makes it harder to predict the best ways to route data and to balance energy consumption throughout the network. Visual sensor networks should have higher bandwidth and support higher data rates in order to support bursty data transmissions with low latency. Therefore, visual sensor networks are constrained with much tighter quality of service (QoS) requirements compared to "traditional" wireless sensor networks. Beside energy awareness, collision avoidance and fault tolerance, additional QoS requirements of visual sensor networks include low data delays, adaptive bandwidth utilization and data priority differentiation.

Considering the limited energy resources and finite radio range of the camera-motes, multi-hop routing remains the preferred method of routing data in visual sensor networks deployed over large areas. In "traditional" wireless sensor networks reactive (on-demand) routing is often used, in order to avoid frequent route updates. However, reactive route discovery and updates introduce additional delays in data routing. Thus, due to the tight demands for low delays, the routes in visual sensor networks must be updated continuously, which requires frequent exchanges of route information between the cameras on current route states.

Since data transmission over the time-varying wireless channel is unreliable, the simultaneous transmission of data over multiple paths significantly can improve data reliability. In [94] Chen et. al. discuss a routing scheme for transmission of real-time video streams over multiple disjoint paths. Multiple routing paths are established based on the proposed directional geographical routing (DGR) algorithm that, combined with FEC coding, provides more reliable data transmission compared to single-path routing, and it achieves better performance in overall delay and quality of video data at the sink. However, although having concurrent data flows increases the data reliability and enables better bandwidth utilization, it also greatly increases transmission cost. Thus, further evaluation is needed to clarify the trade-offs between data reliability and data redundancy in multi-path routing schemes.

Real-time communication is one of the main requirements for networking protocols in visual sensor networks. Delay in packet delivery can be caused by a node's contention for channel access, the node's long packet queues and/or network congestion. The SPEED protocol [43], developed by He et al. is a communication protocol that suits the real-time communication in multi-hop wireless sensor networks, as explained in Section 2.4.5. Since the end-to-end delay in a multi-hop network depends on the distance a packet travels, SPEED routes packets according to the packet's maximum delivery speed, defined as the rate at which the packet should travel along a straight line to the destination. Thus, SPEED determines the transmission delay of the packet considering its end-to-end distance and its delivery speed. However, such a routing scheme is not scalable, as the maximum delivery speed cannot guarantee that the packet will arrive before its delay deadline in larger networks. This issue is addressed in [95], where Felemban et al. propose MMSPEED, where nodes can forward packets with a higher (adjustable) speed if it appears that the packet cannot meet its delay deadline. However, underlying network management policies (discussed in Section 5.8) that regulate nodes' activities have a large impact on the packets' delivery latency. Thus, the data latency problem in visual sensor networks should be further analyzed considering the nodes' resource-aware duty cycling policies.

Furthermore, the networking protocols should support collaboration between camera-motes on various vision-specific tasks. Collaboration-based communication should be established between cameras with overlapped FoVs that, based on the spatial-temporal correlation between their images, reason about the events and thus reduce the amount of data as well as amount of control overhead messages routed through the network [96]. Such a collaboration-based approach for communication is oftentimes used in object tracking applications, where camera-motes are organized into clusters, as described in [97]. Here, the formation of multiple clusters is triggered by the detection of objects. The cluster head node tracks the object, and the cluster head role is assigned to another cluster member once the object is out of the viewing field of the current cluster head. However, in visual sensor networks collaborative clusters can be formed by cameras that have overlapped FoVs, although they can be distant from each other, which can raise questions about the network connectivity. In wireless sensor networks, two nodes are connected if they are able to exchange RF signals. Zhang and Hou [98] prove that if the communication range is at least twice the sensing range, then the complete coverage of a convex area implies that the nodes are connected. However, relation between connectivity and coverage in visual sensor networks still needs to be investigated, considering the fact that 3D coverage needs to be satisfied and that the area of coverage does not necessarily overlap with the transmission range of the camera-mote.

Finally, supporting data priority has a large effect on the QoS of visual sensor networks. Camera-motes that detect an event of interest should have higher priority for sending data over the other cameras-motes. Current protocols for wireless sensor networks focus on minimizing the nodes' active time (the time when a node listens to the channel, transmits or receives a packet), and they support transmissions of small data volumes. Therefore, protocols that provide differentiated service to support prioritized data are needed and must be investigated.

5.10 Hardware Architectures for Visual Sensor Networks

A typical wireless sensor node has an 8/16-bit microcontroller, limited memory, and it uses short active periods during which it processes and communicates collected data. Limiting a node's "idle" periods (long periods during which a node listens to the channel) and avoiding power-hungry transmissions of huge amounts of data keep the node's energy consumption sufficiently small, so that it can operate for months or even for years. It is desirable to keep the same low-power features in the design of camera-motes, although in this case more energy will be needed for data capture, processing and transmission. Here, we provide an overview of works that analyze energy consumption in visual sensor networks, as well as an overview of current visual sensor node hardware architectures and testbeds.

5.10.1 Energy Consumption

The lifetime of a battery-operated camera-mote is limited by its energy consumption, which is determined by the hardware and working mode of the camera-mote. In order to collect data about energy consumption and to verify camera-mote designs, a number of camera-mote prototypes have been recently built and tested. Energy consumption has been analyzed on camera-mote prototypes built using a wide range of imagers, starting from very low-power, low-resolution camera-motes [99, 100], to web cameras [101, 102] to advanced, high-resolution cameras.

An estimation of the camera-mote's lifetime can be done based on its power consumption in different tasks, such as image capture, processing and transmission. Such an analysis is provided in [102], where Margi et al. present results obtained for the power consumption of a visual sensor network testbed consisting of camera nodes built using a Crossbow Stargate [103] board and a Logitech webcam. Each task has an associated power consumption cost and execution time. Measurements of the current for different steady and transient states are obtained. Several interesting results are reported in [102]. For example, in their setup the time to acquire and process an image takes 2.5 times longer than the time to transmit the compressed image. The energy cost of analyzing the image (via a foreground detection algorithm) and compression of a portion of the image (when an event is detected) is about the same as compression of the full image. The authors also showed that packet reception consumes about the same amount of energy as transmission. Finally, they found that transitioning between states can be expensive in terms of energy and time.

In [104] Jung et al. analyze how different operation modes, such as duty-cycle mode and event-driven mode, affect the lifetime of a camera-mote. The power consumption specifications of the camera-mote (which consisted of an iMote2 [105] wireless node coupled with an Omnivision OV7649 camera) consider the power consumption profiles of the main components (CPU, radio, camera) in different operational modes (sleep, idle, working). The generic power consumption model provided in [104] can be used for the comparison of different hardware platforms in order to determine the most appropriate hardware solution/working mode for the particular application.

Considering the fact that data transmission is the most expensive operation in terms of energy, Ferrigno et al. [106] aim to find the most suitable compression method that provides the best compromise between energy consumption and the quality of the obtained image. Their analysis is drawn from the results of measurements of the current consumption for each state: standby, sensing, processing, connection, communication. The authors compare several lossy compression methods, including JPEG, JPEG2000, Set Partitioning in Hierarchical Trees (SPIHT), Sub Sampling (SS) and Discrete Cosine Transform (DCT). The choice of the most suitable compression technique was between SPIHT, which gives the best compression rate and SS, which requires the smallest execution time, has the simplest implementation and assures the best compromise between the compression rate and processing time.

Analysis of the energy consumption of a camera mote when performing different tasks [102] and in different working modes [104] is essential for developing effective resource management policies. Understanding the trade-offs between data processing and data communication in terms of energy cost, as analyzed in [106], helps in choosing the best vision processing techniques that provide data of a certain quality while the lifetime of the camera-mote is prolonged. Analysis of the energy consumption profile helps the selection of hardware components for the specific application. However, the variety of hardware, processing algorithms and networking protocols used in various testbeds makes the comparison of existing camera-motes difficult. Today, there is no systematic overview and comparison of different visual sensor network testbeds from the energy consumption perspective. Therefore, further research should focus on comparing different camera-mote architectures and visual sensor network testbeds, in order to explore the energy-performance trade-offs.

5.10.2 Visual Sensor Node Platforms

Today, CMOS image sensors are commonly used in many devices, such as cell phones and PDAs. We can expect widespread use of image sensors in wireless sensor networks only if such networks still preserve the low power consumption profile. Because of energy and bandwidth constraints, low-resolution image sensors are actually preferable in many applications of visual sensor networks. Table 5.2 compares several prototypes of visual sensor nodes with respect to the main hardware components such as processors, memory, image sensor and RF transceiver.

Compared with processors used for wireless sensor nodes, the processing units used in visual sensor node architectures are usually more powerful, with 32-bit architectures and higher processing speed that enables faster data processing. In some architectures ([100, 108]) a second processor is used for additional processing and control. Since most processors have small internal memories, additional external Flash memories are used for frame buffering and permanent data storage. Image sensors also tends to provide small format images (CIF format and smaller). However, some implementations [67, 108] use two image sensors to provide binocular vision. For example, the Mesheye architecture [67] uses two low resolution image sensors (kilopixels) and one high resolution (VGA) image sensor located in between the two low resolution image sensors. With one kilopixel imager the camera mote can detect the presence of an object in its FoV. Stereo vision from two kilopixel imagers enables estimation

CAMERA-NODE ARCHITECTURE	PROCESSOR	MEMORY	IMAGE SENSOR	RF TRANSCEIVER
MeshEye [67]	Atmel ARM7TDMI Thumb (32-bit RISC), 55MHz	64KB SRAM and 256KB Flash; external MMC/SD Flash	Two kilopixel imagers Agilent Technologies ADNS 3060 30×30 pixels (grayscale) and one ADCM 2700 VGA (color)	Chipcon CC2420 IEEE 802.15.4
Cyclops [100]	Atmel ATmega128L and CPLD - Xilinx XC2C256 CoolRunner	512KB Flash 64KB SRAM	ADCM-1700 Agilent Technology	IEEE802.15.4 compliant (MICA2 Mote [107])
SIMD (Single-Instruction-Multiple-Data)-based architecture [108]	Philips IC3D Xetal (for low-level image processing), 8051 MCU (local host for high level image processing and control)	1792B RAM and 64KB Flash internal on 8051 MCU; dual port RAM 128KB (shared memory by both processors)	VGA Image Sensor (one or two)	Aquis Grain Zigbee module based on Chipcon CC2420
CMUCam3 [109]	ARM7TDMI (32-bit) 60MHz	64KB RAM and 128 KB Flash on MCU, 1MB AL4V8M440 FIFO Frame Buffer Flash (MMC)	Omnivision OV6620, 352×288 pixels	IEEE802.15.4 compliant (Telos mote)

Table 5.2: Comparison of different visual sensor node architectures.

of object position and size, thereby providing the region of interest. Finally, a high resolution image of the region of interest can be obtained using the VGA camera.

It is evident that all camera-mote prototypes shown in Table 5.2 use IEEE 802.15.4 [110] RF transceivers, which is commonly used in wireless sensor nodes as well. The Chipcon CC2420 radio supports a maximum of 250Kb/s data rate, although the achievable data rate is often much smaller due to packet overhead and the transient states of the transceiver. Since such insufficient data rates can be a bottleneck for vision-based applications, future implementations should consider other radio standards with higher data rates, at the cost of increased energy dissipation. Also, by providing a simpler programming interface, the widespread use of visual sensor nodes can be expected. Such an interface is described in [99] where Hengstler and Aghajan present a framework called Wireless Image Sensor Network Application Platform (WiSNAP) for research and development of applications in wireless visual networks. This Matlab-based application development platform contains APIs that provide a user with interfaces to the image sensor and the wireless mote. The WiSNAP framework enables simulations of this visual sensor node platform in different applications.

5.10.3 VSN Architectures – Testbed Research

Testbed implementations of visual sensor networks are an important final step in evaluating processing algorithms and communication protocols. Several architectures for visual sensor networks can be found in the literature.

Among the first reported video-based sensor network systems is Panoptes [101], which consisted of video sensors built from COTS components and software that supports different functions including image capture, compression, filtering, video buffering and data streaming. Panoptes supports a priority-based streaming mechanism, where the incoming video data is mapped to a number of priorities defined by the surveillance application. Panoptes provides storage and retrieval of video data from sensors, it handles queries from users, and it controls the streaming of events of interest to the user. However, the system does not have real-time support — a user can only select to see past events already stored in the system. Also, there is no interaction between the cameras.

In [111], Kulkarni et al. present SensEye – a heterogeneous multi-tier camera sensor network consisting of different nodes and cameras in each tier. The SensEye system is designed for a surveillance application, thus supporting tasks such as object detection, recognition and tracking. These tasks are performed across three network tiers. The lowest layer, which supports object detection and localization, is comprised of Mote nodes [112], and low-fidelity

CMUCam camera sensors. The second tier contains Stargate nodes [103] equipped with web cameras, which are woken up on demand by the camera-nodes from the lower tier to continue the object recognition task. The third tier contains sparsely deployed high-resolution pan-tilt-zoom cameras connected to a PC, which performs the object tracking. The SensEye platform proves that task allocation across tiers achieves a reduction in energy compared with a homogeneous platform, while the latency of the network response is close to the latency achieved by an always-on homogeneous system.

Researchers from Carnegie Melon University present a framework for a distributed network of vision-enabled sensor nodes called FireFly Mosaic [3]. This testbed is illustrated in Figure 5.7. The FireFly platform is built from FireFly sensor nodes enhanced with vision capabilities using the CMUCam3 vision processing board [109]. The CMUCam3 sensor supports a set of built-in image processing algorithms, including JPEG compression, frame differencing, color tracking, histogramming and edge detection. Tight global synchronization throughout the network is supported by using an out-of-band AM carrier current radio transmitter and on-board AM radio receiver. With a synchronization error of $20\mu s$, the system achieves synchronous image capture. The communication and collaboration of camera-motes is scheduled using a collision free, energy-efficient TDMA-based link layer protocol called RT-Link [113]. In order to support camera group communication (among the cameras with overlapped FoVs) both the network connectivity graph (that considers the links between nodes within communication range, shown in Figure 5.8a) and the camera network graph (that considers the relationships between the cameras' FoVs, Figure 5.8b) are considered. In this way cameras that share part of the view, but are out of each other's communication range can still communicate via other nodes. The authors measured the sensitivity of the system's tracking performances, which increases when a larger time jitter is added to the cameras' image capturing time. The size of the transmitted images with a given resolution is controlled by the quality parameter provided in the JPEG standard, which is used for image compression. The authors noticed that JPEG processing time does not vary significantly with the image quality level, but it changes with image resolution, mostly due to the large I/O transfer time between the camera and the CPU. An application of FireFly mosaic includes people monitoring in homes, where the system uses information from cameras with overlapped views in order to define activity regions and merge regions from different cameras.

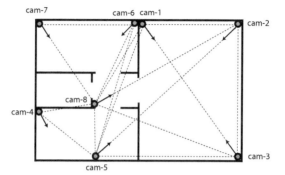

Figure 5.7: Topology of the visual sensor network that is used for testing the FireFly system [3]. The dotted lines represent the communication links between the cameras.

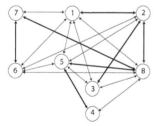

(a) Connectivity graph of the camera-motes from the previous figure. Marked links correspond to the camera network graph.

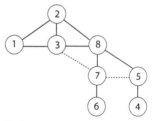

(b) Camera network graph – adjacent links between the cameras indicate that cameras have overlapped FoVs. The dotted lines correspond to the case when the cameras have overlapped views, but cannot communicate directly. The communication schedule must provide message forwarding between these cameras.

Figure 5.8: Connectivity graph and camera network graph of the FireFly system [3].

5.11 Middleware Support

The increased number of hardware and software platforms for smart camera-motes has created a problem in how to network these heterogeneous devices and how to easily build applications that use these networked devices. The integration of camera-motes into a distributed and collaborative network benefits from a well-defined middleware that abstracts the physical devices into a logical model, providing a set of services defined through standardized APIs that are portable over different platforms. In wireless sensor networks, middleware provides abstractions for the networking and communication services, and the main challenges are associated with providing abstraction support, data fusion and and managing the limited resources [114]. In the case of visual sensor networks, the development of middleware support is additionally challenged by the need for high-level software for supporting complex and distributed vision processing tasks. In [115] this support is provided using agent-oriented middleware, where different image processing tasks are carried out by different agents. The agents are responsible for task execution at the processing unit, they can create new agents, and they can remotely create new agents at other cameras, which is fundamental for distributed organization of a smart camera network. In [116], Detmold et al. propose using a Blackboard-based middleware approach instead of the popular multi-agent approach. In this model, the results of processing of input video streams are published at the distributed Blackboard component. Thus, the Blackboard acts as a repository of information, where computations are triggered in response to published results. The Blackboard has several interacting levels. The "single scene analysis" provides information derived from object detection and activity analysis (for example, it produces a "left luggage" hypothesis). The "multi scene analysis" draws conclusions about tracked objects, such as the tracks of people throughout the scene. The "reasoning level" provides higher level hypotheses regarding unusual behavior. Each level contains drivers that process inputs and add them to the level's information space. The information are propagated upwards and shared among the Blackboard levels.

In the future, it is expected that the number of cameras in smart surveillance applications will scale to hundreds or even thousands – in this situation, the middleware will have a crucial role in scaling the network and in integrating the different software components into one automated vision system. In these systems, the middleware should address the system's real-time requirements, together with the other resource (energy and bandwidth) constraints.

5.12 Open Research Problems in Visual Sensor Networks

While extensive research has been done on the many different sub-fields of visual sensor networks, there is still large room for improvement, as discussed throughput this Chapter. Additionally, since the different sub-fields have a strong impact on each other, solutions for many of the remaining open problems can only be found by taking a cross-disciplinary approach that considers all the various aspects of visual sensor networks - vision processing, networking, sensor management and hardware design.

Considering existing work, in most cases there is no coherence between the different aspects of visual sensor networks. For example, networking protocols used in visual sensor networks are mainly adapted from the routing protocols used in traditional wireless sensor networks, and thus do not provide sufficient support for the data-hungry, time-constrained, collaborative communication of visual sensor networks. Similarly, embedded vision processing algorithms used in visual sensor networks are based on existing computer vision algorithms, and thus they rarely consider the constraints imposed by the underlying wireless network.

Embedded vision processing faces challenging problems caused by limitations in the energy, bandwidth and computational resources of the camera-motes. Thus, future efforts should be directed toward finding ways to minimize the amount of data that has to be communicated, by finding ways to describe captured events with the least amount of data. Additionally, the processing should be lightweight – information rich descriptors of objects/scenes are not an option. Hence, the choice of the "right" feature set, as well as support for real-time communication will play a major role in a successfully operated task. In order to keep communication between cameras minimal, the cameras need to have the ability to estimate whether the information they provide contributes to the monitoring task. In a post-event detection phase, sensor management policies should decide, based on known information from the cameras and the network status, whether more cameras need to be included in the monitoring. In addition, data exchanged between camera-motes should be aggregated in-network at one of the camera-motes, and the decision about the most suitable data fusion center should be dynamic, considering the best view and the communication/fusion cost. However, considering the oftentimes arbitrary deployment of camera-motes, where the cameras' positions and orientations are not known, the problem is to find the best ways to combine these arbitrary views in order to obtain useful information.

In the current literature distributed source coding (DSC) has been extensively investigated as a way to reduce the amount of transmitted data in visual sensor networks. In DSC, each data source encodes its data independently, without communicating with the other data sources, while joint data decoding is performed at the base station. This model, where sensor nodes have simple encoders and the complexity is brought to the receiver's end, fits well the needs of visual sensor networks. However, many issues have to be resolved before DSC can be practical for visual sensor networks. For example, it is extremely hard to define the correlation structure between different images, especially when the network topology is unknown or without a network training phase. Also, DSC requires tight synchronization between packets sent from correlated sources. Since DSC should be implemented in the upper layers of the network stack, it affects all the other layers below [117]. Thus, the implementation of DSC will also require careful reconsideration of existing cross-layer designs.

From the communication perspective, novel protocols need to be developed that support bursty and collaborative in-network communication. Supporting time-constrained and reliable communication are problems at the forefront of protocol development for visual sensor networks. Data delays can be reduced when the network is not overwhelmed by data, for example, when extensive processing has greatly reduced the amount of data. However, if a camera-mote acting as a fusion center has to process raw data from several cameras, data latency can significantly increase. By having more fusion centers in the network, latency due to fusion processing decreases since each fusion center processes less data, but the amount of post-fusion data increases. Thus, further research should explore the trade-offs between the ways to combine (fuse) data from multiple sources and latency introduced by these operations.

Multi-hop data communication is another source of data delays in wireless sensor networks. In order to preserve network scalability and to cope with time-constrained communication, there is a need for developing time-aware sensor management policies that will favor utilization of those cameras that can send data over multi-hop shortest delay routes. Such communication should support priority differentiation between different data flows based on priority, which can be determined based on vision information and acceptable delays for the particular data.

The challenging task in visual sensor networks is to minimize the number of undetected or faulty detected events and to provide a reliable response regarding the detected situation. Errors can occur at any moment, either at the camera-mote, during the collaborative reasoning of a group of cameras, or during the data transmissions. At the camera-mote, the information reliability depends partly on the image processing algorithm. For example, consider an object detection algorithm. The algorithm produces an erroneous response when it determines that an object is present when, in fact, it is not, and vice versa. A second source of errors comes from the collaborative processing of images from a group of cameras via multi-sensor data fusion. Finally, errors can also be introduced in transmission of the data over the error-prone wireless channel. Therefore, in order to increase reliability of the system, it is necessary to reduce source of errors in each data-handling block. Only if a system behaves as expected and provides a very small number of faulty alarms will there be a chance that visual sensor networks will be accepted into many vision-dependent applications.

In the future we can expect to see various applications based on multi-media wireless networks, where camera-motes will be integrated with other types of sensors, such as audio sensors, microphones, PIRs, vibration sensors, light sensors, etc. By utilizing these very low-cost and low-power sensors, the lifetime of the camera-motes can be significantly prolonged. However, many open problems appears in such multi-media networks. The first issue is network deployment, whereby it is necessary to determine the numbers of different types of sensors that should be used in a particular application, so that all of the sensors are optimally utilized while at the same time the cost of the network is kept low. Such multi-media networks usually employ a hierarchical architecture, where ultra-low power sensors (such as microphones, PIRs, vibration or light sensors) continuously monitor the environment over long periods of time, while higher-level sensors, such as cameras sleep most of the time. When the lower-level sensors register an event, they notify higher-level sensors about it. Such a hierarchical model (as seen in [111], for example) tends to minimize the amount of communication in the network. However, it is important to reduce the number of false and missed alarms at the low-level sensors, so that the network reliability is not jeopardized. Thus, it is important to precisely define an event at the lower-level sensors, which cameras can interpret without ambiguity. A high-level node acting as a data collector should be able to perform multi-modal fusion of data received from different types of sensors, in order to reason about captured events and decide an appropriate course of action. The reliability of multi-modal data fusion thus depends on the accuracy of the data provided by each sensor modality, so the data from different types of sensors can be associated with different weights before the data fusion.

The growing trend of deploying an increasing number of smart sensors in people's everyday lives poses several privacy issues. We have not discussed this problem in this Chapter, but it is clear that this problem is a source of concern for many people who can benefit from visual sensor networks, as information about their private life can be accessed through the network. The main problem is that the network can take much more information, such as private information, than it really needs in order to perform its tasks. As pointed out in [118], there are several ways to work around this problem. The most radical solution is to exclude cameras from the network, using only non-imaging sensors. However, many situations cannot be resolved without obtaining image data from the area. Thus, the solutions where cameras perform high-level image analysis and provide descriptive information instead of raw images are favorable. The user can be contacted by the system only on occasions when the system is not sure how to react (for example, if an unknown face is detected in the house). In the future, people will most probably need to sacrifice a bit of their privacy if they want to benefit from smart applications of visual sensor networks. However, privacy and security should be seriously addressed in all future designs of visual sensor networks.

Based on the work reviewed in this Chapter, we notice that current research trends in visual sensor networks are divided into two directions. The first direction leads toward the development of visual sensor networks where cameras have large processing capabilities, which makes them suitable for use in a number of high-level reasoning applications. Research in this area is directed toward exploring ways to implement existing vision processing algorithm onto embedded processors. Oftentimes, the networking and sensor management aspects are not considered in this approach. The second direction in visual sensor networks research is motivated by the existing research in wireless sensor networks. Thus, it is directed toward exploring the methods that will enable the network to provide small amounts of data from the camera-motes that are constrained by resource limitations, such as remaining energy and available bandwidth. Thus, such visual sensor networks are designed with the idea of having data provided by the network of cameras for long periods of time.

We believe that in the future these two directions will converge toward the same path. Currently, visual sensor networks are limited by their hardware components (COTS) that are not fully optimized for embedded vision processing applications. Future development of faster, low-power processing architectures and ultra low-power image sensors will open a door toward a new generation of visual sensor networks with better processing capabilities and lower energy consumption. However, the main efforts in the current research of visual sensor networks should be directed toward integrating vision processing tasks and networking requirements. Thus, future directions in visual sensor networks research should be aimed at exploring following inter-disciplinary problems:

- How should vision processing tasks depend on the underlying network conditions, such as limited bandwidth, limited (and potentially time-varying) connectivity between camera-motes or data loss due to varying channel conditions?

- How should the design of network communication protocols be influenced by the vision tasks? For example, how should different priorities be assigned to data flows to dynamically find the smallest delay route or to find the best fusion center?

- How should camera-motes be managed, considering the limited network resources as well as both the vision processing and networking tasks, in order to achieve application-specific QoS requirements, such as those related to the quality of the collected visual data or coverage of the monitored area?

In the end, widespread use of visual sensor networks depends on the programming complexity of the system, which includes implementation of both vision processing algorithm as well as networking protocols. Therefore, we believe that development of middleware for visual sensor networks will have a major role in making these networks widely accepted in a number of applications. We can envision that in the future visual sensor networks will consist of hundreds or even thousands of camera-motes (as well as other types of sensor motes) scattered throughout an area. The scalability and integration of various vision and networking tasks for such large networks of cameras should be addressed by future developments of distributed middleware architectures. Middleware should provide an abstraction of underlying vision-processing, networking and shared services (where shared services are those commonly used by both the vision processing and networking tasks and include synchronization service, localization service, or neighborhood discovery service, for example). By providing a number of APIs, the middleware will enable easy programming at the application layer, and the use of different hardware platforms in one visual sensor network.

Chapter 6

Impact of Routing on Coverage in Visual Sensor Networks

Next we turn our attention to a specific type of wireless sensor network, namely visual sensor networks. As an area with potentially many applications, visual sensor networks impose many new challenges for research. Because the computer vision research area has experienced rapid development in recent years, research on visual sensor networks has been mainly focused on the visual aspects of the network, namely algorithms for image data extraction and analysis. Very little research has been done in order to integrate this knowledge from the vision area and wireless networking for these kinds of systems.

Over the past few years, research efforts in wireless sensor networks have been directed toward the development of efficient routing protocols that minimize energy consumption of the sensor nodes, while meeting certain QoS requirements (such as delay, bandwidth consumption, maximized coverage, etc.) required by the particular application. However, routing in visual sensor networks is still an unexplored field. It may appear that routing protocols developed for wireless sensor networks should behave in a consistent manner regardless of the type of sensors in the network. However, in this chapter we reveal that due to the unique characteristics of visual sensors (i.e., cameras), existing routing protocols applied to visual sensor networks do not necessarily provide the same outcome as when they are used in traditional sensor networks [2].

114

6.1 Introduction

In many applications visual sensor networks must ensure that a monitored area is maximally covered by the cameras in order to provide the required visual information. When a visual sensor network is deployed over a large area, image data captured by the camera-nodes can be routed over multi-hop paths through the network, similarly to the routing of data through "traditional" sensor networks. Since the camera-nodes are powered by batteries, multi-hop routing should help to reduce the overall energy needed for data transmission from the camera-nodes to the data sink. The selection of routing paths through the visual sensor network affects the lifetime of the sensor nodes. Specifically, there are some nodes that are more important to the application than others, such as those cameras that solely monitor some part of the scene. Since the loss of these cameras affects the coverage of the monitored area provided by the camera-network, the selection of routing paths has to be done carefully.

In the Chapter 4, we have shown that sensor nodes may not always be equally important for the particular application. For example, when the application requires maximum coverage over the monitored field, the energy expensive roles should be assigned to the most redundantly covered sensor nodes, so that their eventual loss does not significantly degrade the network's coverage.

We use the knowledge gained about utilizing application-aware role assignment described in the Chapter 4, and we apply it here to visual sensor networks. In the following Chapters we explore the use of application-aware costs for the selection of cameras to transmit data and for the scheduling of sensors to provide full coverage. Specifically concentrating on the routing problem, in this Chapter we analyze how an existing application-aware routing protocol [44] that was initially designed for wireless sensor networks behaves when it is used in a visual sensor network. In particular, we explore two problems essential to visual sensor networks:

- We compare application-aware routing in traditional and in visual sensor networks, for the case when the application requires full coverage of the monitored area.

- We introduce a new cost metric for routing in visual sensor networks, which improves the network's coverage-time compared to the existing application-aware routing cost metrics.

115

6.2 Application-Aware Routing Metrics in Visual Sensor Networks

Among the many applications for visual sensor networks, the interest in telepresence applications has grown significantly in recent times. As we mentioned in Section 5.4, a telepresence system is a system that enables the user to take a virtual tour over a physically remote real world site. For example, the goal of the multidisciplinary project named "Being There" at the University of Rochester is to develop a telepresence system that will enable a user to virtually visit some public area, for example a museum or a gallery.

The "Being There" telepresence system is a network of wireless nodes equipped with very low power cameras. The camera-nodes are mounted at random locations in the room to be monitored. All cameras are identical and static, without the possibility of pan, tilt and zoom. Each camera monitors a finite part of the scene, and the cameras' field of views (FoVs) can overlap, so that images taken from different cameras can be integrated into a complete global view of the scene. Using a control console, a user can navigate and virtually "move" around in the monitored space. Over time, the user expresses a desire to see different parts of the monitored area. Based on the user's requests, the main processing center queries the network in order to retrieve the necessary image data. The query contains the coordinates of the "user request window" (URW) — a part of the scene that is requested by the user.

This application requires three-dimensional coverage of the space. However, this problem is extremely hard to analyze, and some pioneering work has been done in this direction [119]. In order to simplify this problem, initially we assume the task of floorplan monitoring, i.e., monitoring of a scene in one plane. In this task, all camera nodes are mounted in one plane (at the ceiling of the monitored room, for example), and they capture the images of the scene from a parallel plane, as illustrated in Figure 6.1.

We assume that in the first phase of system operations, all cameras with overlapped FoVs are jointly calibrated [79]. Because cameras monitor the scene, which is in one plane, we simplify the problem of volumetric coverage, and consider the coverage of the scene that lies on the plane π_1, as shown in Figure 6.1.

We assume that the camera-nodes s_i are deployed at random locations on the plane π. The physical location of every node on the plane π is represented by coordinates (x, y), and the points of the scene plane π_1 are marked as (x_m, y_m). All cameras are directed toward the π_1 plane, so that the FoV of every camera intersects with plane π_1. Therefore, we can consider that plane π_1 is covered if all points of this plane are covered by the intersection

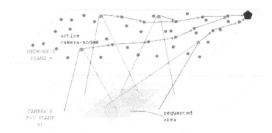

Figure 6.1: Visual sensor network.

the cameras' FoVs and plane π_1.

Instead of sensing and collecting information only from the environment in its vicinity, cameras capture images of distant scenes from a particular direction. Thus, there is a mismatch between the positions of the camera-nodes on the plane π and the positions of the intersections of their FoVs with the observed plane π_1, caused by the different cameras' directions. As a result, it can happen that several cameras that observe the same part of the monitored scene are actually located at distant places from each other. Since the application-aware cost metrics introduced in the Chapter 4 for traditional sensor networks are defined with respect to the positions of the sensor nodes and the positions of their sensing ranges, the displacement of the cameras and their FoVs changes the nature of application-aware routing.

Considering this difference between the sensing abilities of traditional sensors and the cameras, we re-define the application-aware cost metrics introduced in the Chapter 4 in order to adjust them to the case of visual sensor networks.

6.2.1 Application-Aware Cost Metrics for Visual Sensor Networks

Every location (x_m, y_m) on the monitored plane π_1 is characterized by the total energy available for viewing this location:

$$E_{total}(x_m, y_m) = \sum_{s_j:(x_m,y_m)\in C(s_j)} E(s_j) \qquad \forall (x_m, y_m) \in \pi_1, \qquad (6.1)$$

where s_j represents a camera-node, and $C(s_j)$ represents the intersection area of camera s_j's FoV and plane π_1.

Considering the application-aware cost metrics introduced in the Chapter 4, namely *minimum-weight* cost (4.3) and *weighted-sum* cost (4.4), here we define these cost metrics for the case of visual sensor networks.

The minimum-weight cost metric for a camera-node s_i is defined as:

$$C_{mw}(s_i) = \max \frac{1}{E_{total}(x_m, y_m)} \qquad (x_m, y_m) \in C(s_i). \qquad (6.2)$$

The weighted-sum cost metric for a camera-node s_i is defined as:

$$C_{ws}(s_i) = \int_{C(s_i)} \frac{dx_m dy_m}{E_{total}(x_m, y_m)} \qquad (x_m, y_m) \in C(s_i). \qquad (6.3)$$

The energy-aware cost metric C_{ea} (4.7) remains the same in visual sensor networks. Note that up to now, we have defined the C_{mw} and C_{ws} costs using the coordinates (x_m, y_m) on the scene plane π_1. However, the cost of a link between the nodes will depend on the physical positions of the nodes in plane π, assuming that energy spent for packet transmission E_{tx} is a function of the distance between the nodes.

$$C_{link}(s_i, s_j) = C_{aa}(s_i) \cdot E_{tx}(s_i, s_j) + C_{aa}(s_j) \cdot E_{rx}(s_i, s_j), \qquad (6.4)$$

where C_{aa} stands for either the minimum-weight, weighted-sum or energy aware-cost metrics. So, the total cost for routing a data packet from each camera-node s_i to the sink is found as a minimum cumulative cost path from this camera node to the central processing center S_{dst}:

$$C_{route}(s_i) = \sum_{s_i, s_j \in p(s_i, S_{dst})} C_{link}(s_i, s_j) \qquad s_i \in \pi, s_j \in \pi. \qquad (6.5)$$

6.2.2 Selection of Active Cameras

At the beginning of every round, the coordinates of the URW are arbitrarily chosen on the monitored plane π_1. Then, all cameras that cover that part of the scene are determined, as illustrated in Figure 6.1.

For "traditional" wireless sensor networks, the URW area can be covered by several sensor nodes, or for visual sensor networks, with several cameras. Since few nodes can cover the URW completely, the system finds the subsets of the most suitable camera-nodes (those with smallest total costs) that provide the image information from the monitored plane covered by the URWs. The set of active camera-nodes that cover the requested part of the scene

Parameter	Value
Size of the network	$100 \times 100 m^2$
Size of monitored scene	$100 \times 100 m^2$
Bit rate	500 bit/s
Number of nodes	100
Initial energy	2 J
Path loss exponent k	2
Sensing range of a node in traditional sensor network	15 m
Camera's FoV radius	15 m

Table 6.1: Simulation parameters for application-aware routing in a visual sensor network.

with the minimum cost is found by taking into consideration the cumulative costs defined by equation 6.5.

The selection of the camera-nodes is done in the following way. At the beginning of camera selection, all nodes are in the active state. The nodes with higher total routing cost have priority to decide if they will remain in the active state, or they will turn off. The decision is made based on whether all points covered by the camera-node's FoV are covered by other nodes' FoVs with lower cumulative cost.

6.3 Comparison of an Application-Aware Routing Protocol in Wireless Sensor Networks and Visual Sensor Networks

As shown in [44], application-aware routing achieves significant improvement in coverage time, which is the time during which the network is able to preserve full coverage of the monitored area, over energy-aware routing for traditional sensor networks, as shown in Figure 6.2a. However, in visual sensor networks, this routing protocol based on coverage-preserving cost metrics does not preserve the coverage for a longer time compared to energy-aware routing. The results of simulations for visual sensor networks are shown in Figure 6.2b. The simulation parameters are listed in Table 5.1. For example, the C_{ea} metric provides longer time of full coverage compared with C_{ws}, and it outperforms both coverage-preserving metrics, in the case when the network provides almost full coverage (96%). This leads us to believe that

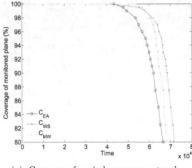

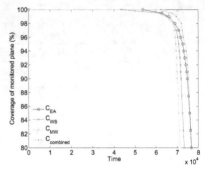

(a) Coverage of a wireless sensor network.   (b) Coverage of a camera-based sensor network.

Figure 6.2: Coverage over time for a traditional sensor network and for a camera-based sensor network for different cost metrics.

this application-aware protocol, which was designed for traditional wireless sensor networks, is not completely applicable to the coverage preserving task in visual sensor networks.

The reason for this result lies in the mismatch between the cameras' physical positions and the cameras' FoVs. For the sake of explanation, we examine the case when a user requests to see a part of the scene on scene plane π_1, as shown in Figure 6.1. The camera-nodes that monitor the requested part can be located anywhere on the camera plane π. Among all the possible camera-nodes that monitor the area of interest, the application-aware algorithm selects the minimum set of camera-nodes with the smallest cumulative cost. Thus, the set of active nodes that cover the part of the area for a minimum cost is chosen from a set of camera-nodes placed at random locations in the network plane π. In the case of traditional wireless sensor networks, the requested part of the scene determines the locations of all sensors that take part in coverage of that part of the scene. In order to preserve coverage, the distance between any two neighboring active nodes can be at most twice the sensing range, which means that the active nodes are grouped together, which is not the case for visual sensor networks.

In application-aware routing, the cost of a node is a function of the available energy of the node, and also of other nodes whose FoVs (sensing ranges) overlap with the nodes FoV. In the case of a traditional sensor network, this cost function tells us how redundantly a sensor is covered, but also evaluates the sensor from the routing perspective. For example, a sensor with low cost is usually a sensor deployed in a dense area, surrounded by many nodes that are equally important as routers and which redundantly cover its sensing area. Therefore, the loss of this sensor will not influence the coverage, nor will it mean the loss of important relaying nodes. In visual networks, however, this cost function values the nodes importance only from the coverage perspective. Although this cost function selects as active nodes the nodes that are more redundantly covered, this selection does not take into consideration the nodes roles as potential routers. For example, it can happen that a camera-node is located in a scarcely-deployed area, so that it is far away from its closest neighbors, but its FoV is overlapped with the FoVs of several other cameras. In an early stage of the network, this camera-node can have an important role as a router, and its energy should not be spent on the sensing task. However, because its FoV is already redundantly covered with that of many other cameras, its cost according to equations 6.2 or 6.3 will be relatively small, which makes it suitable for selection as an active camera for the coverage task.

Among all nodes that cover the requested part of the scene, the applicationaware protocol selects those nodes that have the smallest total cumulative path cost, which is a sum of all the link costs from the node to the sink. On other hand, it is well known that nodes close to the base station are frequently used as routers of data from the other nodes toward the base station and therefore lose their energy much faster compared to the nodes in the rest of the network. However, it is still possible that their FoVs are redundantly covered with the FoVs of other cameras throughout the network, which makes their cost relatively small. Because they are closer to the base station, their total cumulative path cost is in many cases smaller then that of nodes further away from the base station. This makes them suitable for selection as active sensing nodes very frequently. As a result, the loss of these important routers is unavoidable. This speeds up the loss of energy of the rest of the network and makes the "hot spot" problem worse. Therefore, although application-aware routing selects the nodes in the right manner from the coverage perspective, it overlooks the fact that the cameras' FoVs are displaced relative to the camera locations. Thus, when used in a network equipped with cameras, application-aware routing makes energy-inefficient selection of nodes, which leads to loss of a large number of nodes in the early stages of network operation.

In camera-based networks, the energy-aware routing cost surprisingly outperforms the application-aware routing cost in coverage-time. This cost function does not measure a particular node's importance to the coverage application, it only determines the node's ability to be active, based solely on its remaining energy. Although this cost function does not have control over coverage directly, coverage is maintained for a longer time thanks to two factors: the more balanced energy spent among the nodes and the uncontrolled positions of the cameras' FoVs over the monitored area. A node will be selected as an active node if it has more energy than the other potential active nodes, which directly prolongs the lifetime of every node. Over time, the nodes at random locations die across the area, and not necessarily close to the sink, as in the case of the application-aware cost. Due to the unpredicted positions of the cameras' FoVs, the lost coverage due to the death of nodes will also be more or less randomly distributed across the area.

Also, it is interesting to notice that energy-aware routing not only outperforms application-aware routing in the time during which the coverage is preserved, but it also gives, for the same simulation parameters, longer coverage-time when it is used in visual sensor networks compared to the coverage-time in traditional sensor networks. This result can also be explained as a consequence of the uncontrolled positions of the cameras FoVs, and the fact that in each round the active camera-nodes are chosen from a set of nodes that are dispersed over the whole area. This allows the algorithm to choose among nodes with different routing and coverage capabilities, which in turn leads to even more balanced energy spending and more consistent coverage preservation than in the case of traditional sensor networks.

6.3.1 Combined Application and Routing Cost

The simulation results from the previous subsection indicate that the problem of application-aware routing in visual sensor networks is hard to manage in an integrated manner. The results point out that every camera-node should be validated by two separate costs: coverage cost and routing cost. The first cost is related to how important the camera is for covering some part of the monitored area, and the second cost evaluates the importance of the node to act as a possible router of data toward the base station, with the goal of achieving more balanced energy spending over the network. The combined cost for every camera-node can be expressed as a weighted sum of these two cost functions:

$$
\begin{aligned}
C_{combined}(s_j)(\alpha_1, \alpha_2) &= \alpha_1 \cdot C_{ea}(s_j) + \alpha_2 \cdot C_{mw}(s_j) \\
&= \frac{\alpha_1}{E(s_j)} + max \frac{\alpha_2}{E_{total}(x_m, y_m)}, (x_m, y_m) \in C(s_j),
\end{aligned} \tag{6.6}
$$

where α_1 and α_2 are tunable parameters $\{\alpha_1, \alpha_1\} \in [0,1]$ that add weights to the node's routing and coverage capabilities. The lifetime of the visual network with $C_{combined}$ cost used and for different values of α_1 and α_2 parameters is shown in Figure 6.3. The comparison of the results for all cost metrics in coverage-time is shown in Figure 6.2b. The combined cost $C_{combined}$ provides slightly improved results in coverage-time compared with other application-aware costs. It is noticeable that total cost $C_{combined}(0.8, 0.2)$ gives slightly better results than the other cost metrics. With the change in density of the camera-nodes in

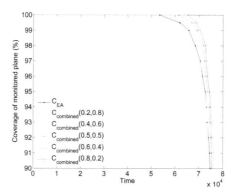

Figure 6.3: Coverage-time of the visual sensor network with the tunable $C_{combined}$ cost metric.

the network, the relationship between the results obtained for different cost metrics remains the same, as illustrated in the Figure 6.4. This figure shows the time for which 95% of the monitored area is still covered by using different cost metrics.

6.3.2   Direct Transmission of Data Packets to the Sink

Although multi-hop transmission of the image data reduces the overall energy consumption of the camera-nodes, it increases the chances for the loss of data due to packet collisions, and it may produce longer packet delays. In scenarios where the sensor network covers smaller indoor areas, in [120] it has been shown that direct transmission of packets to the sink can be a better choice when combined with the appropriate error correction techniques, compared with multi-hop routing.

Figure 6.5 shows the network's coverage-time obtained for the case when the active camera-nodes send their data directly to the sink. Since the data transmission is done over single-hop links, the camera-nodes are chosen based solely on the application cost metrics and energy metrics without considering routing through the other camera-nodes. The results show that when multi-hop routing is not involved, the application-aware metrics outperform the energy aware metric in coverage-time, as is the case for traditional sensor networks. Therefore, in visual sensor networks deployed over small areas (such as in a room, for example), where direct packet transmission is a reasonable choice over multi-hop routing, the coverage preservation metrics introduced in the Chapter 4 can still be used. Once data routing over multi-hop paths becomes necessary, new routing metrics have to be explored.

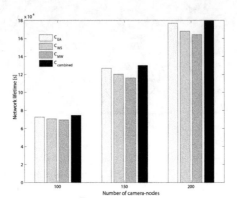

Figure 6.4: Time during which 95% of the monitored area is covered for different numbers of camera-nodes in the network. $C_{combined}(\frac{1}{2}, \frac{1}{2})$ is used in these simulations.

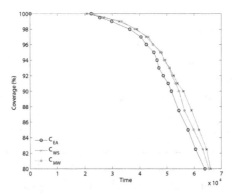

Figure 6.5: Coverage of the camera-based sensor network when active camera-nodes send data directly to the data sink.

6.4 Summary

In this Chapter we have analyzed the case when a coverage preserving routing protocol, which avoids routing through sparsely covered network areas, is used for data routing in a visual sensor network. We found that the camera's unique sensing features can affect the outcome of this routing protocol, which in the case of visual sensor networks does not necessarily provide prolonged coverage over the monitored area compared with the energy-aware routing approach.

The results in this Chapter provide the same conclusion as the results in the Chapter 4, that sensor management and role assignment must be dictated by two goals, coverage preservation and energy balance. In Chapter 4 we saw the importance of considering both coverage and energy when selecting cluster head nodes, active sensors and routers for traditional sensor networks, while in this Chapter we see the importance of considering both coverage and energy in visual sensor networks where the sensing area is disparate from the camera location. In both these cases, the sensors are important to sense the environment (e.g., provide coverage) and to route date (e.g., provide connectivity). Thus, both coverage and connectivity need to be considered in application-aware resource management to extend overall coverage-time of the network.

This work provides only general research directions, and it has room for improvement. For example, we assume that cameras are used as the routers of data through the network. Another interesting scenario would be a heterogeneous network, consisting of camera-nodes that capture images and sensor nodes that act as data routers in the network. In this scenario, an open problem becomes how to decide about the best routing strategy over sensor nodes, such that network resources (bandwidth, energy) are optimally utilized. Also, we assume that every camera-node sends the entire captured image of the monitored area. Since in general several cameras can monitor the same part of the scene, the redundancy in the data collected by these cameras with overlapped FoVs can be very high. In order to reduce the network's demand for energy and bandwidth, each active camera can send to the sink only a part of its captured image, assuming that the main processing center can reconstruct the whole monitored scene from the image parts received from the different cameras. Such an approach that aims to reduce the transmission of redundant data is further investigated in the next Chapter of this book.

Chapter 7

Camera Selection in Visual Sensor Networks

In this Chapter, we examine the selection of camera-nodes in a visual sensor network used in an application whose goal is to provide visual information about a monitored space from any arbitrary viewpoint. The visual sensor network we consider here consists of a large number of randomly placed cameras with overlapped fields of views, which provide images that are synthesized into the user's desired view at a processing center. The selection of a set of the most suitable cameras that jointly provide the user's desired view is one of the basic problems in visual sensor networks [86, 89–92]. As shown in the previous Chapter, this selection must consider both the energy constraints of the battery operated camera-nodes as well as the application's requirement for constant coverage of the monitored space. Therefore, in this Chapter, we propose and compare several methods for the selection of camera-nodes whose data should be sent to a processing center for reconstruction of the user's desired view.

7.1 Collaboration of Cameras

In an energy-constrained and randomly deployed visual sensor network, the choice of the camera-nodes that jointly provide a view of the monitored scene from any viewpoint can greatly affect the network's lifetime and the quality of the reconstructed images [91]. In order to provide images from arbitrary viewpoints over a long period of time, the cameras must *cover* the entire 3D monitored space as long as possible. The definition of coverage in traditional sensor networks, where a point in 2D space is considered covered if it belongs to the sensing range of at least one sensor node, has to be adapted for the case of visual sensor networks. In a visual sensor network, we assume that a 3D point is covered if it is contained in the view volume of at least one camera. When the monitored space is fully covered by the cameras with overlapped views, the images from several cameras can be combined together in order to generate a view from any arbitrary viewpoint.

Similarly to the scenario described in the previous Chapter, we consider here again a visual sensor network based telepresence system that enables the user to take a virtual tour of the place being monitored by the cameras. Each time a user changes position and/or viewing direction, update information is sent back to the system (main processing center), which determines the part of the scene that should be displayed to the user.

In order to generate the images of a scene requested by the user from an arbitrary viewpoint, the main processing center requires the images captured simultaneously by several cameras. In response to a query from the main processing center, each selected camera sends a different part of the user's requested image.

There are several reasons why the cameras should provide only parts of the captured images, instead of the entire images. First, transmission of the redundant parts is avoided, which reduces energy consumption of the camera-nodes. Also, with the currently achievable data rates of the sensor nodes, the transmission of the entire image from each camera-node takes a long time. Therefore, sending only the necessary part of the image from each selected camera reduces the total time needed for obtaining all the image parts at the main processing center. Finally, wireless nodes usually have limited storage space, which may not be sufficient for storing the entire captured image before transmission.

The selection of cameras and the reconstruction (mosaicing) of the user's view from several received image parts requires knowledge of the cameras' characteristic parameters, which can be estimated in the system start-up phase through camera calibration. As described in Chapter 5, camera calibration refers to the process of obtaining the cameras' extrinsic parameters (positions and orientations of the cameras relative to a reference coordinate system) and the cameras' intrinsic parameters. Here, we assume that the relative positions and directions of all cameras are known in advance. Therefore, the quality of the final (mosaiced) image depends on the choice of cameras, the precision of the camera calibration and the algorithm used for image mosaicing.

In this Chapter, we focus on the problem of selecting multiple camera-nodes and combining their images in order to reconstruct a complete view of a part of a planar scene, which corresponds to the user's desired view. Camera selection is performed in two ways. The first camera selection method minimizes the angle between the users's desired view direction and

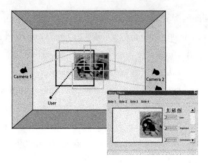

Figure 7.1: Gallery monitoring by a visual sensor network.

the camera's direction. The second camera selection algorithm is based on a cost metric that measures the camera's contribution to the 3D coverage of the monitored space.

7.2 System Scenario

The camera-based network in our scenario consists of the camera-nodes c_m, $m \in 1..N$, mounted on the vertical walls of a room (e.g., an art gallery, as illustrated in Figure 7.1). The locations of the cameras on the four walls, as well as their directions, are chosen randomly. The direction of a camera c is represented by a vector in 3D space $\vec{n_c} = (n_{cx}, n_{cy}, n_{cz})$ that is the camera's optical axis.

We assume that a user is able to "move" through the room, meaning that the user can change position and viewing angle in the room over time. As the user virtually moves through the monitored space, the system periodically receives queries with requests from the user to see a particular view. These queries provide the user's desired 3D location in the room and the direction of the field of view (represented by $\vec{n_u} = (n_{ux}, n_{uy}, n_{uz})$). From the system perspective, a user can be replaced by a *virtual camera* that has the same intrinsic parameters as the cameras used in the system, and an additional ability to change its location and direction (i.e., its field of view) over time.

Our initial scenario assumes that the room monitored by the camera-node system does not contain objects that could partially or fully occlude the view of some cameras. Such a scenario is a simplified version of the more realistic case, when objects appear in the monitored scene. In the absence of objects that occlude the scene, the user's view of an arbitrary scene is just the view of the planar scene from the desired viewpoint. The planar

128

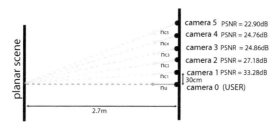

Figure 7.2: Experiment with aligned cameras.

scene is projected onto the user's image plane according to the perspective projection model
of the pinhole camera described in Chapter 5, forming the user's requested view.

For a given position and direction of the user's desired view, there is a group of camera-
nodes that partially share their views with the user's desired view and therefore can provide
images of the scene in response to the user's query. We label this group of cameras as a set
of candidate cameras (CC). Even when a camera observes the same part of the planar scene
as the user's desired view, the image data captured by the camera can be very different from
the image data requested by the user, if the two cameras see the scene under very different
viewing angles. To prevent the selection of these cameras, we only include in the CC set
cameras for which the angle between their optical axis $\vec{n_c}$ and the user's directional view $\vec{n_u}$
is smaller than some threshold angle α_{th}. We label the angle between the user's and camera
c's optical axis δ_{cu} ($\delta_{cu} = \angle(\vec{n_c}, \vec{n_u})$).

7.3 Camera Selection Metrics

As the angle between the directions of a selected camera and the user's desired view δ_{cu}
becomes larger, it is expected that the difference in the image obtained by this camera and
the desired user's image (ground truth image) is larger. In order to evaluate this intuition,
we conducted an experiment with several cameras aligned as illustrated in Figure 7.2. Each
camera captures an image of the planar scene in front. The angle between each camera's
direction and the user's direction (camera 0) increases with the distance of the camera to the
user. We aligned the images taken from each camera to the image taken by the user camera,
by finding the homography mapping [66] between the user's image and each camera's image,
and we measured the peak signal-to-noise ratio (PSNR) of the rendered images, where PSNR
is given by:

129

$$PSNR = 10\log_{10} \frac{MAX^2}{\frac{1}{m \cdot n}\sum_{i=0}^{n-1}\sum_{j=0}^{j-1}\|I(i,j) - K(i,j)\|^2}, \qquad (7.1)$$

where I and K are the original and the rendered image of size $n \cdot m$, and MAX is the maximum pixel value of the image, equal to 255.

We use the same sets of feature points, the projective model and bilinear interpolation of any missing pixels in the reconstruction of the warped images from all cameras. We found that the PSNR of the aligned images does in fact decrease with an increase in the angle between the user's and the camera's viewing directions. Therefore, the angle between the user's and the camera's directions δ_{cu} can be used as an approximate measure of the quality (PSNR) of the reconstructed image.

If the camera-nodes are not constrained by limited energy, the preferable way to select cameras that jointly provide the user's desired image is by choosing those cameras that contain different parts of the scene a user is interested in, and that have the smallest angle between their directions and the user's direction. However, since the camera-nodes are battery-operated, this camera selection method should be modified so that it considers the remaining energy of the camera-nodes as well. Also, another constraint for camera selection comes from the fact that the monitored space is non-uniformly covered (monitored) by the cameras.

The non-uniform coverage of the 3D space is the result of the random placement of the camera-nodes on the walls, which results in parts of the 3D space being out of reach of any camera, and parts that are monitored by a number of cameras at the same time. The cameras' visible volumes are overlapped, so that the volume of one camera can be partially or fully contained in the visible volume of other cameras. In the absence of objects, the scene viewed by a camera may be recovered from the images taken by the cameras with overlapping views. Such a camera is redundantly covered, and its loss will not prevent a user from seeing the part of the scene that is covered by this camera.

On the other hand, the situations when the system loses the "important" cameras, those that solely monitor some part of the space, can be prevented (delayed) when the selection of the active camera-nodes is done based on a metric that combines information about the remaining energy of the camera-node with information of how redundantly each camera's visible volume is covered by the rest of the cameras. Since this metric does not consider the angle between the directions of the selected camera and the user, it is expected that the images from the cameras selected based on this metric differ more from the image expected by the user, compared to images obtained from the cameras selected based on the "minimum

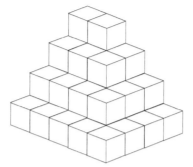

Figure 7.3: Voxels — basic elements for volumetric representation of the monitored space.

angle" method.

Based on these observations, we introduce two methods for the selection of cameras: camera selection based on the smallest angle between the user's and the camera's direction, and camera selection based on a 3D coverage cost metric, which considers the remaining energy of the camera nodes as well as the redundancy in the coverage of the 3D space that belongs to the camera's view volume. This last cost metric is similar to the application-aware cost metrics used in the previous Chapters.

7.3.1   Camera Selection Based on Minimum Angle

In this minimum angle selection approach, the most suitable cameras to provide the desired image are chosen by minimizing the angle δ_{cu} between the camera's axis and the user's view direction. Although this method is straightforward and it minimizes the distortion between the reconstructed image and the desired image, there is a drawback — it does not consider the importance of the camera-node to the task of coverage preservation over the monitored space. Thus it causes a premature loss of the nodes important to the monitoring of areas that are not redundantly covered by other camera-nodes' viewing volumes.

7.3.2   Camera Selection Based on Volumetric Camera Cost (VCC)

In order to define this cost metric, we use a volumetric description of the scene, which is a concept commonly used in 3D computer graphics for the reconstruction of a scene or an object based on joint consideration of all cameras' available views. In the simplest case, the monitored space is divided into small equidistant cubical elements called voxels [73], as shown in Figure 7.3. Each voxel can belong to the visible volume of several cameras, or it may not be included in any camera's visible volume, in which case the 3D space represented by this voxel is considered uncovered by the visual network.

Knowing the positions and the directions of the cameras and their fields of view, for each voxel we can find the group of cameras that contain this voxel in their view volumes. If each camera-node has remaining energy $E_r(c_m)$, $m \in 1..N$, we can find the total energy of each voxel as the sum of the remaining energies of all the cameras that contain this voxel:

$$E_{total}(v(i,j,k)) = \sum_{\{c_m|v(i,j,k)\in VV(c_m)\}} E_r(c_m), \tag{7.2}$$

where $v(i,j,k)$ is the center of the voxel, and $VV(c_m)$ is the visible volume of camera-node c_m.

The volumetric camera cost (VCC) measures the camera's importance to the monitoring task, and it is defined as the sum of the energies of all voxels (defined in equation 7.2) that belong to this camera's viewing volume:

$$C_{VCC}(c_m) = \sum_{v(i,j,k)\in VV(c_m)} \frac{1}{E_{total}(v(i,j,k))}. \tag{7.3}$$

7.3.3   Direction Based Volumetric Camera Cost (DVCC)

The information captured in the image depends on the camera's direction. Although the cameras can share the same 3D space, the information content of their images may be completely different. For example, two cameras on opposite walls can have overlapped visible volumes, but they image completely different scenes. Based on this observation, we can define a direction dependent volumetric camera cost metric (DVCC), which considers not only the fact that the cameras share the same visible volume, but also whether or not they view the scene from similar viewing directions. In other words, the volumetric cost metric of a camera c_m can be modified so that the new cost metric considers only those cameras that share the same 3D space with this camera and for which the angle between their direction and this camera's direction is smaller than 90°.

For every camera c_m, $m \in 1..N$, we can find a subset of the cameras that satisfy these requirements, labeled as $Sc(m)$. Now, each camera's cost depends only on the remaining energy of the cameras from $Sc(m)$, and not on the remaining energies of the nodes from the entire network. Therefore, as seen from camera c_m, the total energy of the voxel $v(i,j,k)$ is equal to the energy of all cameras from the subset $Sc(m)$ that contain this voxel:

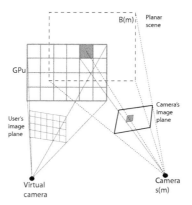

Figure 7.4: Camera selection.

$$E_{total}(v(i,j,k))\{m\} = \sum_{\{c_t|v(i,j,k)\in VV(c_t),c_t\in Sc(m)\}} E_r(c_t). \tag{7.4}$$

The direction based volumetric cost of the camera is thus:

$$C_{DVCC}(c_m) = \sum_{v(i,j,k)\in VV(c_m)} \frac{1}{E_{total}(v(i,j,k))\{m\}}. \tag{7.5}$$

7.4 Algorithms for Camera Selection

The low-power camera-nodes are envisioned to have the ability to send only a part of the captured image instead of the entire image. Using inputs from the user about the desired view's position and direction, the main processing center runs a camera selection algorithm and determines the set of active cameras along with the specific image parts needed from each active camera. The main processing center then queries each selected camera-node for that part of the image, which represents communication overhead. However, this additional communication is in turn paid off by a significant reduction in the energy needed for the transmission of only the required image part, instead of the entire image.

In order to determine the required parts of the image from each camera, the image plane of each camera is projected onto the plane (wall) in front of the camera, bounding the part of the planar scene that can be observed by the camera, as illustrated in Figure 7.4. These visible scene parts from each camera are labelled as B_m, $m \in \{1..N\}$. Visible regions of the scene are found only once, at system start-up, since the cameras do not change their direction and location over time.

The image plane of the user is divided by a grid into equal size blocks of pixels. Based on the current position and direction of the user, the system calculates the 3D coordinates of the grid points located on the user's image plane, as well as the coordinates of the user's image plane projections onto the plane (wall) that the user currently sees. The cells of the projected user's grid onto the wall are labelled as GPu. For each cell from GPu the system can find a set of camera-nodes from CC that contain this grid cell in their visible region B_m.

We provide an algorithm that selects the final set of cameras together with the parts of their images that must be sent back to the main processing center. Additionally, we modify this algorithm for the case when the selection is made based on the "minimum angle" criteria, considering the changes in the viewing angles of the camera and the user across the planar scene.

7.4.1 Region Based Camera Selection Algorithm (RBCS)

Using any of the proposed cost metrics as a criteria for camera selection, the main processing center determines the set of cameras that take part in the reconstruction of the user's desired view. From all cameras in CC that see a part of the scene the user is interested in, the region based camera selection (RBCS) algorithm first chooses the camera c with the smallest cost. Then, RBCS determines all the grid cells from GPu that are contained in the viewing region B_c of this camera. This subset of grid cells from GPu is then mapped back to the camera image plane, determining the region of the image captured by camera c that will be transmitted back to the main processing center. All cells from GPu that belongs to the viewing region B_c of this camera are mapped as covered. For the rest of the still uncovered cells from GPu, RBCS repeats the same procedure. The algorithm stops once when either all the cells of the user's projected grid GPu are covered or there are no more cameras from CC that can be considered by this algorithm.

7.4.2 Block Based Camera Selection Algorithm (BBCS)

The camera selection algorithm described in the previous Section is simple to implement, but when the cameras are chosen based on the "minimum angle" criteria, the camera selection algorithm described in the previous Section has to consider a perspective projection of the scene onto the cameras' image planes. According to this model the angle between a ray from

134

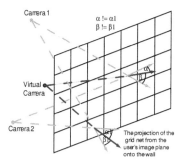

Figure 7.5: A change in the viewing direction of the camera and the user across the planar scene, considered for the BBCS algorithm.

the camera to some point on the user's projected grid and a ray from the user to the same point changes over the planar scene (wall), as illustrated in Figure 7.5.

The block based camera selection (BBCS) algorithm determines the parts of the images needed by taking this fact into account. BBCS finds the best camera from the set of candidate cameras CC for each cell from GPu individually. Among all cameras that contain this cell from GPu in their field of view, BBCS chooses the camera-node with the smallest angle between the ray that passes from the camera through the center of this cell and the ray from the user to this cell's center.

7.5 Simulation Results

We preformed simulations for 10 different scenarios with the proposed camera selection metrics and for both camera selection algorithms (RBCS and BBCS). Each scenario uses a visual network of 40 camera-nodes, mounted on the four vertical walls of a room of size $10 \times 10 \times 4$ meters. The positions and directions of all cameras are chosen randomly. We assume in the simulations that the selection of the camera-nodes, which together reconstruct the user's desired view, is repeated in every iteration, where in each iteration the user moves to a different position in the room. The cameras provide images with a resolution of 320×240 pixels, and the horizontal viewing angle (field of view) for all cameras is equal to $40°$. The image plane of the user is divided into blocks of 8×8 pixels. We assume that the energy needed for transmission of an image part from the camera node to the processing center is proportional to the size of the transmitted image part.

Figure 7.6a shows how the coverage of the monitored 3D space changes over time for different cost metrics using the block based camera selection (BBCS) algorithm. This figure shows the percentage of all voxels that are in the view volume of at least one camera-node and therefore are considered covered according to our definition of coverage in 3D space introduced in Section 7.1. The simulations show that over time, a larger part of the 3D monitored space is considered covered when the VCC or the DVCC costs are used to find the set of cameras, compared with using the "minimum angle" metric. Since both the VCC and the DVCC metrics consider whether the view volume of a camera is covered by the view volumes of other cameras, these metrics direct the camera selection algorithm to avoid the selection of cameras that are not redundantly covered, thus prolonging the lifetime of these high cost camera-nodes. Also, as the camera-node's remaining energy gets smaller, the cost of the camera-node increases significantly, again with the purpose of keeping the camera-node from being selected as an active node whenever the selection algorithm can find another suitable camera.

In order to estimate the quality of the reconstructed image, we measured the average angle δ_{cu} between the user's direction and the direction of the selected cameras. This is plotted in Figure 7.6b. Using "minimum angle" as a criteria for camera selection the images are on average less warped compared to the images from the cameras selected based on the VCC or the DVCC metrics. The smaller angle δ_{cu} between the user's direction and the selected cameras' directions means there will be a smaller difference in the images provided by these cameras compared to the ground truth image. Thus, by combining the results provided in Figures 7.6a and 7.6b, we can see that there is a clear trade-off in the time during which the monitored space is completely covered by the visual network, and the quality of the reconstructed images requested by the user of this system.

Figure 7.7 shows the results of the simulations performed for the case when camera selection is done by using the region based (RBCS) algorithm. The simulation results for the RBCS algorithm are similar to the results for the BBCS algorithm. Both the VCC and DVCC metrics outperform the "minimum angle" metric in terms of prolonging coverage of the 3D space over time, but the "minimum angle" metric chooses cameras that provide images closer to the user's desired image, as can be seen from 7.7b. Although RBCS requires less computation than BBCS, BBCS provides more accuracy in determining the set of required cameras based on the "minimum angle" criteria.

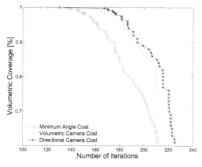
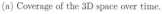

(a) Coverage of the 3D space over time.

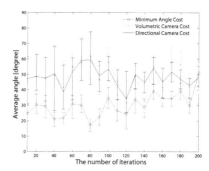

(b) Average δ_{cu} between the user's direction and the directions of the selected cameras.

Figure 7.6: Simulation results for the different cost metrics used for camera selection based on the BBCS algorithm. $\alpha_{th} = 90°$

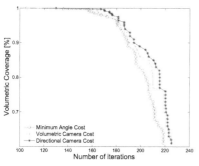

(a) Coverage of the 3D space over time

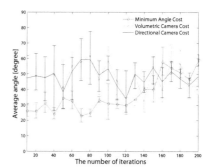

(b) Average δ_{cu} between the user's direction and the directions of the selected cameras.

Figure 7.7: Simulation results for the different cost metrics used for camera selection based on the RBCS algorithm. $\alpha_{th} = 90°$

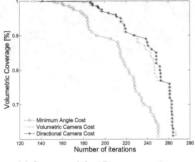

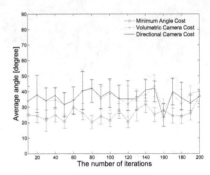

(a) Coverage of the 3D space over time.

(b) Average δ_{cu} between the user's direction and the directions of the selected cameras.

Figure 7.8: Simulation results for different cost metrics used for camera selection based on the BBCS algorithm. $\alpha_{th} = 60°$

7.5.1 Influence of α_{th} on 3D Coverage

The simulation results discussed in the previous Section are obtained for the case when the set of cameras CC is chosen based on threshold angle $\alpha_{th} = 90°$. For smaller values of α_{th}, the average angle between the cameras' and the user's direction gets smaller, as can be seen by comparing Figure 7.6b with Figure 7.8b where the angle α_{th} is set to 60°. By comparing these figures, we can see that the 3D coverage is preserved for a longer period of time when α_{th} has a smaller value.

To explain these results, we compare the total amount of data obtained at the main processing center. We find that once the coverage drops below 100%, for smaller α_{th} it happens more often during the simulations that the user's image cannot be fully reconstructed, since the camera selection has fewer choices of cameras among which it selects a set of active cameras. In the case of smaller α_{th} the cameras on average send less data to the main processing center, as can be seen from Figure 7.9, which shows the total number of pixels of the reconstructed image at the main processing center, for the BBCS camera selection algorithm and for different values of the threshold angle α_{th}. Since the selected cameras produce less data, on average they spend less energy over time, which is the reason for the prolonged coverage over time compared with the case when α_{th} is equal to 90°.

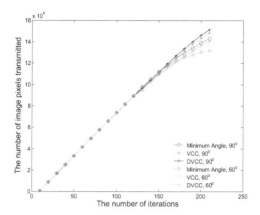

Figure 7.9: Comparison of the average number of data pixels sent to the main processing center from all selected cameras for the cases when $\alpha_{th} = 60°$ and $\alpha_{th} = 90°$ and BBCS camera selection algorithm.

7.5.2 Camera Direction Dependent Coverage

The previous results show that the DVCC metric achieves slightly better performance in terms of prolonged coverage over the 3D space compared to the VCC metric. The DVCC metric is derived from the VCC metric, but it only considers those cameras whose visible volumes' share the same 3D space and also point in a similar direction in the space. This metric more specifically determines the cost of the camera-node, since it considers the fact that the information content from the camera's image depends on the camera's direction, so that cameras that share the same information content should have smaller cost, and vice versa.

Following this logic, every camera-node can measure the 3D coverage of the space in its view volume from its direction. Since the measurement of the 3D coverage from each camera's direction is complex, we measure the direction dependent 3D coverage in the following way. The directional coverage represents the percentage of the space (in terms of voxels) that is seen by at least one camera-node from a certain direction. We choose four directions in the room, which correspond to the normals of the four walls of the room. All cameras are thus divided into four groups, where each group is represented by one direction, as shown in Figure 7.10. The cameras choose their groups according to the angle between their directions and the group direction. Each group of cameras observe the monitored space from a different

Figure 7.10: The cameras are divided into the four groups, depending on their directions.

direction, and each of them see different facets of the voxels. Remember that for the purpose of calculating the VCC and DVCC cost metrics, the 3D space of the room is divided into voxels, and each of the four vertical facets of the voxel can be best seen by the cameras from one group. We measured the percentage of the voxels' facets contained in the field of view of at least one camera from each group of cameras, and for the purpose of comparison, we performed the same simulations for the case when camera selection is done based on the VCC cost and the "minimum angle" criterion.

The results for this directional based 3D coverage are shown in Figure 7.11, for two arbitrarily chosen groups of cameras (the cameras from each group see the 3D space from one main direction). Since the information content of the images depends on the cameras' directions, the 3D coverage can be seen as a measure of the amount of 3D space covered by the cameras from certain directions. Therefore, the 3D space not only needs to be covered by the cameras, but it also has to be covered uniformly from all possible directions, and the DVCC metric can be used to achieve this.

7.5.3 Comparison of 2D and 3D Coverage

We measured the percentage of covered area of the walls in the monitored room over time for the different cost metrics, which actually corresponds to the coverage of the 2D area. This represents the case when we are interested only in prolonging the time during which the visual network can fully monitor the walls, which is a special case of the coverage of the 3D space. In Figure 7.12 we present results for 2D coverage, i.e., coverage of the planar scenes, with various cost metrics. As is the case for 3D coverage, we see that both the VCC and the DVCC metrics achieve better results in prolonging coverage time compared with the "minimum angle" metric.

140

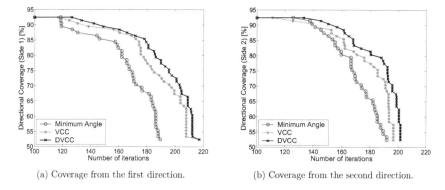

(a) Coverage from the first direction.   (b) Coverage from the second direction.

Figure 7.11: Directional coverage: coverage measured for two arbitrarily chosen directions and with different cost metrics and the BBCS algorithm.

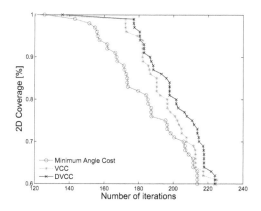

Figure 7.12: 2D coverage measured over the monitored planes, for different cost metrics.

7.6 Reconstruction of the User's Desired Image

Upon reception of the image parts from the selected camera-nodes, the main processing center maps these image parts to the virtual image plane of the user, and it stitches the image parts together. There are several types of error that can occur in the final image. There is geometric error due to the mis-alignment of the pixels from the camera images compared to the pixels in the desired image. This mis-alignment error depends on the precision of the camera's estimated parameters. Differences in the intensity of the pixels across the final image can also occur due to the variance in the intensity levels of the images taken by cameras from locations in the room with different lighting conditions. Another type of error that can occur is due to the different distances of the cameras to the user's desired planar scene, which basically affects the resolution of the final image. The cameras that are close to the requested plane provide images of higher resolution compared to those that are further away.

In this Section, we present the results of an experiment with 7 cameras. The goal of this experiment is to mosaic the image parts obtained from the cameras that are chosen based on different camera selection metrics into the final image. The cameras are placed in one plane, and they point toward the observed plane. We use the BBCS algorithm to select the set of active cameras.

Figure 7.13a shows the mosaiced image from the cameras that have the most similar directions with the user. Figure 7.13b shows the same reconstructed user's view, generated from the cameras that have the smallest volumetric cost. By visually comparing these two images with the reference image obtained from the user's position (Figure 7.13c), we can notice that the second image (Figure 7.13b) has more distortion than the image in Figure 7.13a, due to different lighting conditions of the chosen cameras that lie further away from each other. However, this result is provided for illustrative purposes only, and it presents only a rough estimation of the quality of the final images obtained by both metrics.

7.7 Quality Estimation of the Reconstructed Images

Results in the previous Section show us that there is a clear trade-off in the network coverage-lifetime and the quality of the reconstructed images. Therefore, in this Section we address this lifetime-quality trade-off by measuring the PSNR (peak signal-to-noise ratio) of the reconstructed images obtained in simulations with the different camera selection metrics introduced in Section 7.3.

(a) Cameras selected based on the "minimum angle" criteria.

(b) Cameras selected based on the volumetric camera cost (VCC).

(c) Reference image—the user's desired image.

Figure 7.13: The user's desired image obtained by mosaicing the images parts from the cameras selected by the "minimum angle" and the volumetric camera cost metrics.

This set of simulations is performed with 36 cameras that monitor a 3m × 4m plane. The VCC metric introduced in equation 7.3 is adapted to the case of plane scene monitoring, such that it depends only on the coverage of the monitored planar scene. This cost metric is already provided in equation 6.3 in the previous Chapter, and here it is labelled as the maxCOV metric. The PSNR of the reconstructed images obtained for the maxCOV and "minimum angle" costs are compared with the PSNR of the image that is reconstructed by using the maxPSNR metric, defined next.

The maxPSNR metric is defined in the following way [121]. For each block of the user's viewpoint (defined in Section 7.4), the views from the cameras that contain this block are transformed and compared with the ground truth image. The camera that provides the highest PSNR of this block is then selected to send this part of the final image to the processing center. The maxPSNR cost cannot be used in a real camera system, since the ground truth image is not available. However, maxPSNR gives us an upper bound on the PSNR of the reconstructed image that can be achieved by the cameras in the system.

The coverage-time obtained by the different cost metrics is shown in Figure 7.14c, while the corresponding PSNR of the reconstructed images is shown in Figure 7.14a. As expected, at the beginning of the simulations, the maxPSNR cost provides the highest PSNR among all the metrics, outperforming the coverage cost by about 3dB and the "minimum angle" cost by about 1dB. However, with the "minimum angle" and maxPSNR costs, the network loses the ability to provide full coverage compared with the coverage cost metric. The drop in coverage (after around 40 simulation rounds for "minimum angle" and around 65 rounds for maxPSNR) is followed by a sharp drop in PSNR, leaving the coverage cost to provide better coverage and better PSNR after this point.

Figure 7.14b shows the PSNR values of the reconstructed images in a scenario when all cameras have infinite sources of energy. The cameras selected by the three metrics provide full coverage of the monitored plane. Here, maxPSNR provides the best quality images, as expected, with a PSNR that is about 3dB larger than the coverage cost and about 1dB larger than the "minimum angle" cost. Figure 7.14 clearly demonstrates the trade-off in the quality of the reconstructed images and the coverage-time obtained by different camera selection methods. Finally, a snapshots of the reconstructed images obtained using the

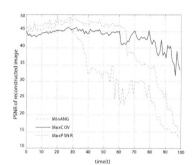

(a) PSNR of the mosaiced images.

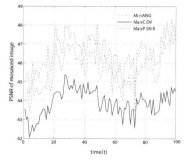

(b) PSNR of the mosaiced images, in case of cameras with the infinite energy.

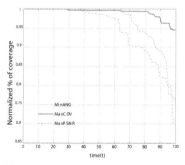

(c) Normalized percentage of coverage of a target plane over the number of rounds (time).

Figure 7.14: Coverage-time and PSNR obtained through simulations.

(a) Real image.

(b) Mosaiced image using "minimum angle" cost, PSNR = 43.956dB.

(c) Mosaiced image using coverage cost, PSNR = 43.432dB.

(d) Mosaiced image using maxP-SNR cost, PSNR = 45.053dB.

Figure 7.15: Snapshots of images rendered in the simulations.

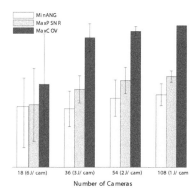

Figure 7.16: The total energy of 108J is allocated to different numbers of camera-nodes.

different camera selection methods are shown in Figure 7.15.

7.8 Energy Distribution in Visual Sensor Networks

Here we explore the impact of allocating a fixed amount of energy (108J) among different numbers of camera-nodes (18, 36, 54 and 108) on network lifetime. We measure the time for which the camera-network covers at least 95% of the target plane. Figure 7.16 shows the network lifetime obtained for different allocations of the energy in the network.

By increasing the number of cameras, the energy is more evenly distributed throughout the monitored space, and thus the network lifetime is prolonged. The coverage metric (max-COV) outperforms the other two metrics in all cases. The variances in network lifetime for all three metrics decrease when more cameras are used. Thus, by increasing the number of cameras, the network lifetime is not only prolonged, but the uncertainty in lifetime obtained by the different metrics is reduced.

7.9 Camera Selection in the Presence of Objects

In the previous Sections we assumed that the monitored space does not contain any objects, which simplifies the camera selection problem. However, in many real situations it is common to have objects in the scene. In such cases the problem of camera selection becomes much more complicated. The problem is how to deal with occlusions since the view of some cameras may be occluded and therefore they cannot contribute to the reconstruction of the desired view.

In this Section we extend our work on camera selection for the case when the monitored space contains a moving/static object. Our approach for the reconstruction of a full image of this non-planar scene assumes separate image reconstruction of the object and its background [122]. Depending on the particular application, we can use different methods to select the cameras that provide the desired view of the object and its background, which affects the lifetime of the camera network.

Camera selection in the presence of occluding objects has already been studied in the literature. An heuristic approach for camera selection that minimizes the visual hull of the objects is shown in [80], for example.

We assume that a network of fully calibrated cameras is able to detect and to locate an object present in the monitored scene [73]. In the simplest case, the detected object can be approximated by a bounding box around the object. The network provides a view of the scene from a certain direction by combining (mosaicing) [66] images from several cameras into one output image The goal of such a visual sensor network is to reconstruct the full view of the room monitored by the cameras, by providing a complete view of the room's walls as well as each side (plane) of the bounding box around the object.

Such a camera-based network can be used for different surveillance tasks, such as object tracking or object recognition, for example. As illustrated in Figure 7.17 these tasks may require images of an object and the background taken with different resolution. For example, for object recognition, the network should provide high quality (high resolution) images of the captured object, while the image quality of the background can be reduced. This is similar to the foveated vision phenomena, where human eyes focus on the details of a specific object, thereby providing less information about the object's background.

In the previous Sections we defined two methods for selecting cameras that provide images used for reconstructing an image captured from a user-specified view point and direction. The minimum angle selection method provides images of higher quality compared to DVCC. We concluded that these two camera selection methods provide a trade-off between the quality of the reconstructed image (measured as peak-signal-to-noise ratio - PSNR) and the network's ability to cover the monitored space for an extended period of time. Our aim now is to show how these camera selection methods can be utilized for the reconstruction of a view of a monitored space in the presence of occluding objects.

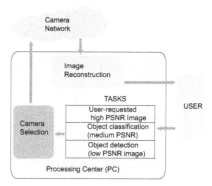

Figure 7.17: Task-specific selection of cameras in a visual sensor network.

7.9.1 Reconstruction of Scene View

Since an object in the scene is approximated by its bounding box, each side of the box is a plane. Therefore, the reconstruction of the full view of the room includes the reconstruction of the view of every plane (box side) and the reconstruction of the object's background. Depending on the application-specific task, the MPC uses different methods for selecting cameras to cover the box's sides and visible parts of the object's background. For object recognition, for example, selection of cameras that provide images of the object can be done by using the minimum angle selection method, since it provides images of higher PSNR compared to DVCC. On the other hand, selection of cameras that provide images for reconstruction of the background can be done based on DVCC. Cameras selected by this method usually provide lower resolution images, but at the same time this method prevents early loss of cameras that non-redundantly cover some part of the monitored space.

7.9.2 Simulation Results

In order to analyze how these combined camera selection methods affect the time during which the camera network provides (almost) full coverage of the monitored space (measured as a percentage of the monitored space covered by at least one camera's viewing frustum), we simulate a camera-based network consisting of 40 cameras randomly placed on the walls of a room of size $10 \times 10 \times 4m$. An object (approximated by a bounding box) is placed in the middle of the room. We used several combinations of the two selection methods (listed in Table 7.1) to obtain images of the bounding box planes (object) and the background scene.

Application/Method	Object	Background
Highest resolution	Min. angle	Min. angle
Object recognition	Min. Angle	DVCC
Object detection	DVCC	DVCC

Table 7.1: Combined methods for camera selection in the presence of an object in the scene.

In each simulation round a complete view of each side of the room with the captured object is reconstructed with respect to the user's position and direction that was chosen at the opposite side of the room. Each selected camera spends energy that is proportional to the part of the image it provides.

As shown in Figure 7.18, coverage-time of a visual sensor network changes when using different combinations of camera selection methods. In the case when the application does not require high quality images (e.g., when object and background images are reconstructed by using images from cameras selected using DVCC) coverage-time of the visual sensor network can be up to 30% longer compared to the coverage-time of a network that always has to provide the highest quality reconstructed (mosaicked) images (e.g., when both the object and the background are reconstructed from images of cameras chosen by the minimum angle selection method).

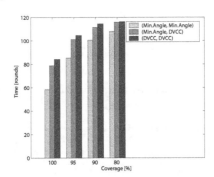

Figure 7.18: Coverage-time of the camera network.

7.10 Summary

In this Chapter, we reviewed our work on different camera selection methods in visual sensor networks. Cameras are selected to provide the image data necessary for the reconstruction of the planar scene from any arbitrary viewpoint. Also, we analyze the way to reconstruct the final view in the case when an object is present in the monitored area. Our proposed metrics for selecting cameras provide a trade-off between the network lifetime and the quality of the reconstructed images.

In the future we will focus on extending the proposed work on the camera selection in two direction. First, we want to further investigate the camera selection problem in the event-based visual networks, where the camera activity depends on the registered event of interest. Furthermore, we want to incorporate the bandwidth allocation problem in the camera selection. By allocating the bandwidth among the cameras, we assure that cameras with higher priorities provide data, and we can control the amount of data coming from each camera. Therefore, by incorporating bandwidth allocation to the cameras we can further optimize the utilization of the visual sensor network resources.

Chapter 8

Camera Scheduling in Visual Sensor Networks

Sensor scheduling is one of the basic strategies for effectively using the limited sensor battery power in wireless sensor networks [123, 124]. The aim of sensor scheduling is to decrease redundant sensing in the network, and therefore to minimize the energy spent by the sensor nodes. In the case of visual sensor network, the capturing and transmitting of images taken by a number of cameras requires a significant amount of energy. However, continuous monitoring of a physical space can often be successfully performed by using only a subset of camera-nodes, while allowing the other cameras to enter a low power sleeping mode. These subsets of active camera-nodes should be changed over time in order to balance the energy spent among all the nodes in the network. Therefore, in this Chapter we discuss the advantages of using scheduled sets of camera-nodes in a visual sensor network.

First, we will provide an overview of the scheduling problem of sensor nodes in a wireless sensor networks, and then, we will continue with exploring the scheduling problem of camera-nodes in a visual sensor network used for a specific user-centric application.

8.1 Energy Efficient Scheduling of Sensor Nodes

The formal definition of the problem of how to find energy-efficient schedules in a wireless sensor network was first introduced in [125]. Given a monitored region R, a set of sensor nodes $s_1, .., s_n$, sensing regions of the sensor nodes $R_{s1}, .., R_{sn}$ and their energy supply $b_1, .., b_n$ the problem is to find a monitoring schedule $(CS_1, t_1)..(CS_k, t_k)$ where CS_i is a *sensor cover set* and t_i is the time associated with CS_i, such that $\sum_{i=1}^{k} t_i$ is maximized, while the energy

Algorithm 2 The Garg-Könneman algorithm applied to sensor networks.

1: *Initialize* : $\delta = (1 + \epsilon)((1 + \epsilon)N)^{-\frac{1}{\epsilon}}$ *for* $i = 1, .., N$ $y(i) \leftarrow \frac{\delta}{E(i)}$, $D \leftarrow N\delta$, $j = 0$

2: **while** $D < 1$ **do**

3:     $j \leftarrow j + 1$,

4:     *Find the column* j, *the cover set with the minimum length$_y(j)$*

5:     *Find row* p, *the index of the sensor* s_i *with the minimum* $\frac{E(p)}{P_A(p,j)}$

6:     $t(j) \leftarrow \frac{E(p)}{P_A(p,j)log_{1+\epsilon}\frac{1+\epsilon}{\delta}}$

7:     $\forall i = 1, .., N$, $y(i) \leftarrow y(i)(1 + \epsilon \frac{E(p)}{P_A(p,j)} \setminus \frac{E(i)}{P_A(i,j)})$

8:     $D \leftarrow E^T y$

9: **end while**

consumption of each sensor node s_i does not exceed its battery reserves b_i.

The scheduling problem can be formulated as a linear packing problem, defined by the linear program:

$$max\left\{ \mathbf{c}^T \mathbf{x} | \mathbf{A}\mathbf{x} \leq \mathbf{b}, \mathbf{x} \geq 0 \right\}. \tag{8.1}$$

Since the number of columns of $\mathbf{A}$ (which corresponds to the number of cover sets) increases exponentially with the number of sensors, the approximative solution of this problem is based on the $(1 + \epsilon)$ Garg-Könemann [126] algorithm. This algorithm finds the column j of $\mathbf{A}$ by minimizing the so-called length defined as $length_y(j) = \frac{\sum_i A(i,j)y(i)}{c(j)}$ for any positive value of vector $\mathbf{y}$ (shown by Algorithm 2).

Finding the cover sets and time schedule of sensor nodes using the Garg-Könemann algorithm requires that elements of matrix $\mathbf{A}$ be set as:

$$A(i,j) = \begin{cases} P_A & \text{if sensor } s_i \in CS_j \\ 0 & \text{if sensor } s_i \notin CS_j , \end{cases} \tag{8.2}$$

where P_A is the power spent by a sensor node while active. Vector $\mathbf{x}^T$ represents the time schedule $t_1, .., t_k$ of cover sets $CS_1, .., CS_k$, vector $\mathbf{b}^T$ contains sensor nodes' initial battery energies and vector $\mathbf{c}$, in the case of equally weighted sensor nodes, is set to the vector of positive constants.

The Garg-Könemann algorithm solves the scheduling problem by using a subset of all columns (cover sets) of matrix A, thereby extending the sensor network lifetime close to the optimal solution (within a factor of $(1 + \epsilon)$ from the optimal solution). Parameter ϵ controls the fidelity of the solution since with a decrease in ϵ the number of cover sets grows fast, which enables the network lifetime to more closely approximate the optimal solution.

8.2   Power Management through Camera Scheduling

The energy consumption of a camera-node is dominated by the energy consumption of the main hardware components: processor, image sensor (camera) and radio. Depending on its current task, the camera-node enters different operational modes – active, idle and sleep, while spending different amounts of energy in each mode. To reduce energy consumption while still providing coverage of the monitored space, we consider the case when a group of different sets of camera-nodes $\hat{C}S = \{C_s(1), .., C_s(m)\}$, which provide full coverage of the monitored region, is used over time. In such a scenario the camera-nodes from the currently active set $C_s \in \hat{C}S$ monitor the space of interest while the remaining camera-nodes enter the low-power sleep mode.

There are several reasons for using scheduled camera-node sets for a continuous monitoring task:

- In this book, we deal with user-centric visual sensor networks, where the network's response (image data sent from the camera-nodes) depends on the user's query (defined by the user's virtual position and direction in the monitored space). Since the moment when a user's request arrives cannot be predicted, the network needs to have cameras ready to respond to the request at any time.

- Visual sensor networks designed for applications that require images from any viewing direction (such as target tracking or event-triggered applications) should continuously monitor the space of interest. In this case a group of cameras should be able to provide images at every time instance.

- Some applications may require that a camera-network continuously collect and store the images over time – in this using a minimum number of cameras that provide full coverage significantly reduces the required storage space compared to the case when all cameras are always turned on.

8.2.1   Camera Scheduling in Visual Sensor Networks

There are several differences between the scheduling of camera-nodes in a user-centric visual sensor network and the scheduling of nodes in a traditional sensor network:

154

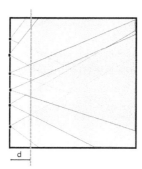

Figure 8.1: The cameras cover the monitored space starting from a distance d from the wall.

- The sensing model has to be adapted from a 2D model in the case of sensor networks to a 3D model in the case of visual sensor networks.

- In order to reduce energy consumption image sensors can be designed to select a part of the captured image [127], which is then transmitted over the wireless channel.

- Based on the current user's request to see some part of the scene, a group of camera-nodes from the currently active camera-node set C_s will be chosen to reply to the user's query. It is not possible to predict the user's requests (a part of the scene that the user is interested to see) over time in a user-centric visual sensor network. Thus, we cannot find the optimal schedule for the camera-node sets. However, using camera-nodes organized in multiple cover sets still provides significant energy savings compared to the case when all camera-nodes are always turned on over time.

Therefore, we discuss a heuristic approach for camera-node scheduling in a visual sensor network and provide results of camera-node scheduling in the case when the network serves multiple users over time.

8.2.2 Scheduling Model

In the previous Chapter we emphasized the importance of having the monitored space covered by the cameras from all directions for the longest period of time. However, due to the cameras' anisotropic FoV the space very close to the cameras is not fully covered by the cameras' fields of view. Therefore, considering the cameras' FoVs (as illustrated in Figure 8.2)

155

we assume that the space from each direction should be covered by the cameras' FoVs starting from some distance d from each wall.

Since the camera-nodes mounted on different walls monitor the space from different directions, the scheduling of the four groups of camera-nodes GC^i, $i = 1, .., 4$ is performed separately. To find the group of the cover sets $\hat{CS}^i$ for each group of camera-nodes GC^i, we divide the monitored space into cubical elements (voxels) of the same size. Using the Garg-Könemann algorithm we find a finite number of camera-node cover sets $\hat{CS}^i, i = 1, .., 4$ for each group of camera-nodes. Each camera-node set $C_s \in \hat{CS}^i$ covers all voxels that are at a distance d or greater from this group of cameras.

Time is divided into *scheduling frames* T_{sf}. On every wall the camera-nodes from one cover set $C_s^i \in \hat{CS}^i, i = 1, .., 4$ monitor the space during one scheduling frame. After every communication round T_{sf} the MPC decides whether to change the current camera-node cover set C_s^i. The set C_s^i from $\hat{CS}^i$ with the highest total remaining energy becomes the active camera set in the following T_{sf}.

The main processing center (MPC) manages the network's resources. It receives information from the camera-nodes on their remaining energies, and based on this information the MPC updates the cameras' coverage costs (given by equation 7.5) and selects the cameras that should provide images as a response to the user's query. The group of camera-nodes that are selected from the current cover set C_s^i is labelled as C_a^i.

To assure collision-free transmission of the data packets, the communication between the selected camera-nodes and the MPC is organized according to a time division multiple access (TDMA) model. Time is divided into communication rounds called *response frames* (as illustrated in Figure 8.2), where during each response frame the selected camera-nodes send image data to the MPC. The response frame begins with a control packet broadcast by the MPC that informs all camera-nodes in currently active camera-node sets $C_s^i, i = 1, .., 4$ about the selected camera-node C_a^i that have to send their image data back to the MPC. The control packets from the MPC carry information about the order in which selected camera-nodes must reply back to the MPC, as well as information about the parts of the images that each camera-node has to transmit. After the control packets are broadcast, the uplink communication begins, where selected camera-nodes transmit their images back to the MPC.

The duration of one response frame T_{rf} varies over time, as it depends on the number of selected camera-nodes and the amount of data that each selected camera-node transmits back to the MPC. Thus, T_{rf} corresponds to the time needed to send N_{cp} control packets from

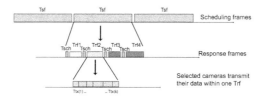

Figure 8.2: Scheduling of the camera-nodes in a visual sensor network. One cover set C_s^i is used during one scheduling frame. Selected cameras C_a^i transmit their image in one time slot of T_{rf}.

Mode	CPU	Radio	Camera	Total
Active – P_{tx} [mW]	6	52.2	60	118.2
Active – P_{rx} [mW]	6	59.1	60	125.1
Idle [1] P_{idle}[mW]	6	0.003	60	66.003
Sleep P_{sleep} [μW]	3	3	30	36

Table 8.1: Power consumption of a camera-node at 0dB Tx power. The camera-node consists of a Tmote Sky mote with an Omnivision OV6130 camera.

the MPC to the camera-node plus the time needed to send data packets from all selected camera-nodes to the MPC over a wireless channel.

8.2.3 Energy Model

We use a simplified energy model that accounts for the energy consumption of three main camera-node components: CPU, radio and image sensor. The camera-node consists of a TMote Sky [33] wireless sensor node coupled with an Omnivision OV6130 image sensor [128]. Depending on its activity over time, each camera-node changes between different states, where the main components (CPU, radio, image sensor) enter different working modes (active, idle, sleep). Following the power consumption model for camera-node presented in [104] each working mode is characterized by the power consumption given in Table 8.1.

The MPC selects a group of camera-nodes from the current set C_s^i based on a user's request. The MPC then assigns to each selected camera-node c_j a duration $T_{tx}(j)$ during which the selected camera-node should transmit its data back to the MPC. All other camera-

---

[1]Note that the idle mode of a camera-node assumes that the radio is in sleep mode.

nodes from the current cover set C_s^i remain in idle mode. The camera-nodes that do not belong to the current cover set C_s^i are in sleep mode during the time T_{sf}. The energy consumption of camera-nodes that are selected to capture images (E_A), those in idle mode (E_I) and those in sleep mode (E_S) during one communication round are:

$$E_A(j) = P_{rx}T_{sch} + P_{tx}T_{tx}(j) + (T_{rf} - T_{tx}(j))P_{idle}, \forall j \in C_a^i \tag{8.3}$$

$$E_I(j) = P_{rx}T_{sch} + T_{rf}P_{idle}, \forall j \notin C_a^i \tag{8.4}$$

$$E_S(j) = (T_{sch} + T_{rf})P_{sleep}, \forall j \notin C_s^i, \tag{8.5}$$

where T_{sch} is time required to send the control packets from the MPC, and $T_{rf} = \sum_{\forall c_k \in C_a^i} T_{tx}(k)$.

Parameter Name	Symbol	Value
Number of cameras	N	80
Room size	A	$10 \times 10 \times 4$ m
Scheduling frame	T_{sf}	30 s
Number of control packets/size	N_{cp}	2/30 bytes/packet
Initial battery energy	E	50 J
Data rate	R	250 kb/s
Data/payload size of packet	p	74/64 bytes
Image sensor QCIF resolution	SR	288×352 pixels
Image resolution	IR	8 bits/pixel

Table 8.2: Parameters used in the simulations of the camera-node scheduling.

The camera-node sets $C_s^i \in \hat{C}S^i$ are changed over time either after time T_{sf} or in the case when any of the camera-nodes in the currently active set dies. Further explanation regarding the camera-node set scheduling is provided in Algorithm 3.

8.2.4 Camera Selection based on Minimum Cover Cost

The camera-node selection procedure for this visual sensor network application is described in the previous Chapter, Section 7.4.1. The user's image plane is divided into blocks of equal sizes. The MPC selects for each block one camera with the smallest coverage cost (defined by

Algorithm 3 Scheduling algorithm applied to the camera-nodes.

1: $Initialize : Find\ set\ of\ feasible\ camera - node\ cover\ sets\ \hat{CS^i}, i = 1,..,4\ using$
$Garg - K\ddot{o}nemann\ algorithm.$

2: $T_s^i = 0,\ i = 1,..,4$

3: $Start\ simulations :$

4: **while** $\exists c \in N \mid E_{rem}(c) > 0$ **do**

5:     $Select\ set\ of\ camera - nodes\ C_a^i\ i = 1,..,4\ to\ respond\ to\ user's\ query$

6:     $T_s^i = T_s^i + T_{rf}^i,\ i = 1,..,4$

7:     $Selected\ camera - nodes\ C_a^i\ transmit\ data\ to\ MPC.$

8:     $\forall i, i = 1,..,4\ check :$

9:     **if** $E(c) == 0,\ c \in C_a^i$ **then**

10:        $Find\ Cd,\ Cd = \{C_s^i \mid c \in C_s^i\}$

11:        $\hat{CS^i} = \hat{CS^i} \setminus Cd$

12:        **if** $\hat{CS^i} = \{\}$ **then**

13:           $Find\ set\ of\ feasible\ cover\ sets\ \hat{CS^i}, i = 1,..,4\ using\ Garg - K\ddot{o}nemann$
$algorithm.$

14:        **end if**

15:     **end if**

16:     **if** $T_s^i > T_{sf}$ **then**

17:        $C_a^i \longleftarrow \tilde{C}_s^i,\ \tilde{C}_s^i \in C_s^i$ $-set\ with\ the\ highest\ remaining\ energy$

18:        $T_s^i = 0$

19:     **end if**

20: **end while**

---

equation 7.5) that contains this block in its FoV. The block is then perspectively projected onto the selected camera's image plane. This determines the part of the image that the selected camera must transmit back to the MPC.

In order to reduce communication between the MPC and the selected camera-nodes, the required image part from the selected camera is determined by two coordinates: the upper left pixel (P_{start}) and the lower right pixel (P_{stop}) of the requested image part, as illustrated in Figure 8.3. For each selected camera these coordinates are broadcast in the control packets at the beginning of each scheduling frame. Therefore, the part of the image transmitted to the MPC contains pixels that are required for the reconstruction of the user's view as well as overhead pixels. This overhead can be arbitrarily large, and it increases with the

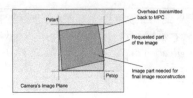

Figure 8.3: The requested image part contains useful pixels and pixel overhead.

number of cameras. Therefore one of the tasks of the MPC is to minimize this overhead by selecting fewer camera-nodes while still selecting camera-nodes with small coverage costs. Beside energy efficiency, smaller communication overhead results in a shorter time needed to respond to the user's request.

Therefore, we modify the camera-node selection algorithm presented in Section 7.4.1 so that it aims to select the set of camera-node based on the total minimum cost. We call this algorithm Minimum Cover Cost (MCC). The algorithm is presented in Figure 8.5.

8.2.5 Simulation Results

The results of our simulations confirm the advantage of using the MC algorithm over the case when the selection of camera-nodes is based only on the cameras'individual costs denoted as Cost-based Camera Selection (CCS).

Using the MCC algorithm, the number of selected camera-nodes over time is smaller than by using CCS, as shown in Figure 8.5a. This results in a smaller amount of overhead data transmitted by the selected camera-nodes. Additionally, this results in shorter query response time (shorter T_{rf}), as illustrated in the Figure 8.6a.

Since the time needed to respond to a user's query is shorter, the camera-nodes from C_s^i spend less time in idle mode and thus they waste less energy. Therefore, using the MCC algorithm the camera-nodes are able to respond to more queries over the network lifetime. Figure 8.7a presents the number of reconstructed images at the MPC from data received from the camera-nodes that are selected using the CCS and MCC algorithms. Here we assume that camera-nodes transmit the image parts requested by the MPC. The total number of reconstructed images (which corresponds to the number of user's query responses) until the network loses 95% of the nodes is $15 - 20\%$ higher using MCC compared to using CSS.

We also compared the MCC and CCS algorithms in the case when camera-nodes do not have the ability to select the image part but instead have to transmit the entire captured

For each group of camera-node GC^i, $i = 1, .., 4$:

1   Find all camera-nodes from the currently active camera-node set C_s^i that cover some part of the user's requested image (label them as C_m^i).

2   Find all camera-node sets (labelled as MS^i) from C_m^i that maximally cover the user's requested view (using Garg-Könemann algorithm).

3   Assign the cost $sCost^i(m)$ to each cover set $ks_m \in MS^i$ calculated as:

$$sCost^i(m) = \sum_{\forall c(j) \in ks_m} C(j), \; \forall ks_m \in MS^i$$

where $C(j)$ is the current coverage cost of camera $c(j)$

4   Select the set of camera-nodes that has the smallest cost $sCost^i$ among all sets. These camera-nodes will provide the user's requested image.

Figure 8.4: Minimum Cover Cost (MCC) algorithm.

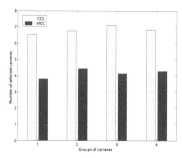 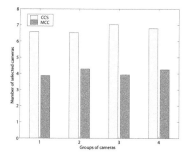

(a) Selected cameras provide a part of the image to the MPC.

(b) Selected cameras transmit the entire captured image to the MPC.

Figure 8.5: The average number of selected cameras in one communication round for each room side, for the CSS and MCC algorithms. The camera network serves one user during its lifetime.

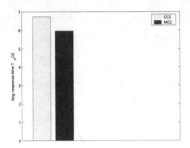
(a) Selected cameras send a part of the captured image to the MPC.

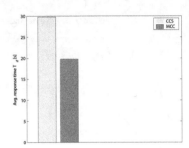
(b) Selected cameras transmit the entire captured image to the MPC.

Figure 8.6: The average duration of one response frame T_{rf}. The camera network serves one user during its lifetime.

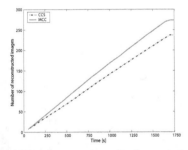
(a) Selected cameras transmit only a part of the image to the MPC.

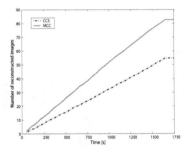
(b) Selected cameras transmit the entire captured image to the MPC.

Figure 8.7: The total number of reconstructed user's views until 95% of all cameras in the network die.

image to the MPC. The improvement provided by MCC over CCS is even better. The number of selected camera-nodes (given in Figure 8.5b) is similar to the case when camera-nodes transmit image parts (Figure 8.5a), but the average query response time is much longer than in the previous case (Figure 8.6b). Since the selected camera-nodes transmit more overhead data with CCS, MCC improves the total number of responded queries by around 45% compared to CCS (Figure 8.7a).

8.3 Query-Merging for Multiple Users

The user-centric visual sensor networks we consider should be accessible on-line by multiple users at the same time. Thus the system should be able to process multiple users' queries simultaneously.

The network's response time (the time for which the network provides the images needed for reconstruction of the desired users' views) is bounded by the maximum achievable data rate in the network. In order to prevent long queues of users, requests from multiple users should be merged together in order to serve them efficiently. Therefore, a high QoS for such a network assumes that all users are provided with the desired view with a small delay while the network spends minimum resources (energy, bandwidth) to reply to all users.

Let us assume that there are N_u users who simultaneously request images from different arbitrarily chosen view points. The MPC divides the users' image planes into blocks that are projected on the walls. For each projected block the MPC finds all camera-nodes from the currently active camera set C_s^i that contain this block in their FoV.

The MPC then "merges" all queries in the following way: it finds all feasible sets of cameras that cover all users' blocks. Then, it chooses the set of cameras with minimum total cost using the MCC algorithm. The camera-nodes from the chosen set C_a^i provide image data that is used for reconstruction of the final images for multiple users. This is basically the MCC algorithm used in the case of multiple users (MCC-MU).

We compared MCC-MU with the case when the set of active cameras C_a^i is chosen only based on the cameras' costs (CCS-MU). In this case, we are still using data from one camera in the reconstruction of multiple users' views, but we do not try to minimize the number of cameras in the chosen set C_a^i.

We simulate the cases when the system serves 1,3,5,7, and 10 users simultaneously. Figure 8.8a shows the total number of reconstructed users' images for different numbers of users in the system. A smaller amount of overhead data, as in the case of the MCC algorithm,

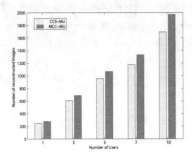

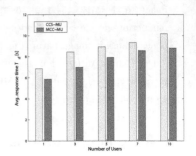

(a) The average number of reconstructed images at the MCP until 95% of all cameras die, in the case of multiple user queries.

(b) The average response time to the multiple-user query.

Figure 8.8: Simulation results for the case of a network that serves multiple users' queries simultaneously.

results in a higher number of reconstructed users' views at the MPC over time. Also, the performance of MCC-MU depends on the overlap of the users' views – higher redundancy (overlap) in the users' views enables that fewer cameras be used to transmit all image data to the MPC.

Figure 8.8b shows the average T_{rf} for different numbers of users. As expected, the time needed to receive all image data from all selected cameras is always shorter with MCC-MU compared with CSS-MU.

8.4   Summary

In this Chapter we analyzed the scheduling problem of the camera-nodes in a user-centric visual sensor network. This analysis is application-specific considering the fact that the system has to provide images from some predetermined part of the scene. We concluded that in order to minimize the time of the network's response to the user and to minimize energy consumption, it is necessary to engage the minimum number of cameras that support all requests. Such an approach leads to a higher number of satisfied users' queries in a visual sensor network that serves either a single user or multiple users.

In general, the cameras can be scheduled to transmit data according to TDMA model (as shown in this Chapter), or by following the contention-based model. Each approach has its own advantages and drawbacks. For example, with TDMA-based medium access, the collisions of packets are avoided, but tight synchronization is necessary throughout the visual sensor network. By the contention-based model, each camera has the ability to send the data immediately upon the captured event, however, the chances of packet collisions also increase. Therefore, our future work will be concentrated to the comparison between the TDMA approach and contention-based approach for camera managing in the visual sensor networks.

Chapter 9

Precise Positioning via WSN and Image Data Integration

Localization, which provides a sensor node with information about its physical position in a network, is one of the most fundamental services that has to be supported by a wireless sensor network for almost any application. Simply, collected data from the sensor nodes becomes meaningless without the information about where this data comes from. The location information is not only required for characterizing collected data, but it is needed for other purposes as well. For example, many routing algorithms are based on the assumption that the locations of the sensor nodes are already known, or that these locations can be easily obtained (for example, with the help of GPS, or by some localization algorithm). Coverage preserving algorithms and metrics, such as those presented in this book, are also dependent on information about the location of the nodes in the network. In many applications, including those for tracking moving objects, monitoring an intruder's attack or responding to alarm situations, information about the location of the sensor nodes is crucial for the correct performance of the application.

Although location information is essential in many sensor network applications, obtaining highly precise location information is extremely hard due to several reasons, such as unreliable signal strength measurements (caused by unpredictable changes in the wireless channel's condition), changes in the network's topology caused by the loss of nodes, etc. Various location estimation methods have been proposed so far, such as those based on measurements of received signal strength (RSS), angle of arrival, and time of flight. Also, different technologies, such as infrared and ultrasound technology, have been explored to be used alone or in combination with RF signals for positioning systems.

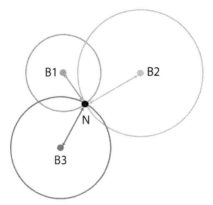

Figure 9.1: Localization based on tri-lateration.

In this Chapter, we present a prototype of a positioning system that provides precise coordinates of a moving object. The system utilizes information from a set of beacon nodes with known locations and, by measuring the signal strength of the received signal, it finds a rough position of the moving object. Using the information extracted from a camera's images of the moving object, the system is able to refine the estimated coordinates of the object. However, in order to recognize the object from the image, the object has to be marked with a visible marker. Once the object is captured by the camera, the marker is detected and the fine-scale position of the object is obtained, the system is able to track the moving object as long as the marker is visible to the camera. This positioning system for high precision location estimation is very robust, and it can be used in many applications, such as robot localization, control and navigation or tracking of the assets in warehouses or hospitals.

9.1 Related Work on Localization Systems

Localization assumes finding the distance of a node with an unknown location relative to nodes located at known positions. There are several common approaches for estimating the distance between two nodes [129]. Time-based methods record the time of arrival (ToA) or time-difference-of-arrival (TDoA). Knowing the propagation speed of the signal (such as RF, acoustic, infrared or ultrasound), the propagation time can be translated into the distance between the two nodes. Angle-of-arrival (AoA) methods use the angle at which the signal is received and geometry to estimate the node's position.

A common approach used to find the positions of the sensor nodes in a network is based on measurements of the strength of the received signal (RSS) from several reference nodes placed at known locations (we refer to these nodes as beacons). After receiving messages from at least three beacon nodes, the moving node can use tri-lateration and easily calculate its current position, as illustrated in Figure 9.1. Tri-lateration is a basic localization mechanism that uses the distances between three points with known locations and the point at the unknown location to calculate the unknown position as the point on the intersection of circles centered at the known points [130]. This approach is based on the fact that an RF signal propagates through an isotropic environment, with signal strength decreasing with distance from the sender. However, in real situations, the signal is usually attenuated on its way from the sender to the receiver, due to many factors, such as diffraction from objects, shadowing, scattering, etc. Such a received signal does not obey the model by which the RSS is simply a function of the distance from the sender. The environmental influence on the strength of the received signal is hard to model, and it is almost impossible to predict the signal strength at the receiver. However, many localization methods assume an RF signal travels through an ideal medium and arrives at the receiver unchanged. This becomes a source of error in the positions estimates. Therefore, solutions that incorporate some sort of statistics about the error in estimated distances to the point with unknown coordinates, or solutions that consider the measurements from more reference points have been explored as well. Positioning algorithms usually give better results in outdoor environments than in indoor environments, since the signal in an indoor environment is exposed to many changes due to diffraction from objects and walls on its way to the receiver.

Since almost all applications of sensor networks require location information, this research area is very attractive and it has been the center of interest for a while. The proposed solutions are numerous and versatile since each solution is built for a particular application. In this Section, we give a short overview of several interesting location systems based on different technologies and methods used for location calculations.

GPS (Global Positioning System) [131] is among the first location systems to make a breakthrough in industry and the consumer market, but due to its high cost and inability to provide precise position information in indoor environments, it is not a viable solution for localization within a sensor network.

The RADAR system [132] is a localization system designed for an indoor environment. It uses RF signal strength measurements from three base stations in order to track the location of a user. The measurements of the signal strength are first collected across multiple positions within a room in the offline phase to produce a set of signal strength maps. In the second phase, these maps are used for comparison with the signal strength from the user station, which should alleviate the multipath effects.

Another indoor localization system is Cricket [133], which uses the difference in the arrival times of RF and ultrasound signals to determine the position of the node in the space.

SpotOn [134] is another location system that is based on measurements of signal strength to provide the localization of the wireless devices. The positions of the nodes are estimated relative to each other rather than to any fixed infrastructure of beacon nodes.

AHLoS (Ad Hoc Localization System) [130] provides a distributed localization method that requires only a limited fraction of nodes (beacons) to know their exact locations, while other nodes can dynamically discover their locations through a two-phase process, ranging and estimation. During the ranging phase each node estimates its distance from its neighbors, while in the estimation phase, nodes use the ranging information and known beacon locations to estimate their position. Once a node estimates its position, it becomes a beacon node and it assists other nodes in estimating their positions.

MoteTrack [135] is a robust, decentralized RF-based location system, which we use in our work, discussed later. Location estimation in this system is based on empirical measurements of the radio signal from multiple transmitters, similar to the RADAR location system. The difference between them is that MoteTrack is a signature-based localization system, which means that the position estimate of a tracked node is done by acquiring signatures, messages from beacon nodes with known positions, and by comparing these signatures with a reference signature database. In general, the system consists of a set of beacon nodes that periodically broadcast beacon messages, which consist of tuples in the form (*sourceID*, *powerLevel*). *SourceID* is a unique identifier of a beacon node, and *powerLevel* is the transmission power level used to broadcast the message. The system has to be installed and calibrated before use. In the offline phase, a collection of reference signatures is acquired manually by a user with a laptop and a radio receiver. The reference signature is collected by the node at a known location and consists of a set of signature tuples in the form (*sourceID*, *powerLevel*, *meanRSSI*), where *meanRSSI* is the mean received signal strength collected from a set of beacon messages. For robustness of the system, the database with collected reference signatures is replicated across the beacon nodes. In the online phase of the system, a moving node receives periodic beacon messages and computes its signature, which it sends to the beacons, thereby requesting information on its location. One or more of the beacon nodes compute the signature difference between the node's signature and their reference signature database, and they send the signature difference back to the node, which then computes its location information.

Some initial work that utilizes a camera's information to find the precise position of a target has already been reported. For example, [136] describes a system architecture that provides location information and tracking of a moving target that carries a tag that emits near infrared signals, which can be received by the camera module. An FPGA connected to a camera is used for processing the rough data from the cameras and for implementation of the real-time tracking algorithm.

Easy Living [137] is a system developed by Microsoft for tracking multiple people in a room. The system uses Triclops stereo cameras that provide the positioning capability in a home environment, and the color images are used to maintain the people's identities. A background substraction algorithm and depth estimation using the stereo vision is used to locate 3D blobs in each camera's field of view, which are then merged to provide the people's shapes. However, with more than three people moving around, the system is not able to provide good results, since the frequent occlusions cause poor maintenance of the coherent tracks of the people.

In this Chapter we present a positioning system that obtains precise locations of a moving object by integrating information from a network of wireless nodes with known locations and one camera. The prototype of the system described here has been developed and fully tested at Siemens Corporate Research Center, Princeton NJ.

9.2   System Description

The proposed system for fine position estimation and tracking of a moving target in an indoor environment [138] is shown in Figure 9.2. The system consists of several parts, which communicate to the central server that collects the data, controls the system operations and estimates the precise position of a tracked object.

As illustrated in Figure 9.2, the main components of the system are:

- *Real time wireless sensor network based positioning system* — this system consists of a set of reference wireless sensor nodes (beacons), which are mounted on the ceiling of a room at known locations. We have used MoteIV TMote Sky wireless nodes [139] for the implementation of a testbed with the MoteTrack location system, which is described in Section 9.1. However, any location system based on a wireless sensor network can be used here as well. Prior to system start up, we collect information about the signal

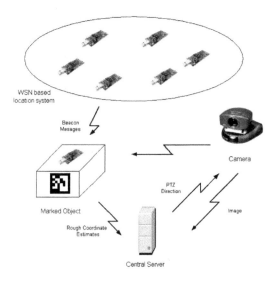

Figure 9.2: Positioning system based on a WSN and a single camera.

strength (called radio signatures) from the beacon nodes across multiple positions within the room. The radio signatures are then stored on the beacon nodes, forming a distributed signature database. Since the radio signatures are collected over many positions, the reliability of the estimated coordinates of the moving target increases.

- *Pan-Tilt-Zoom IP camera* — we used a Sony EVID-30 IP camera, which was connected to the server. The central server periodically receives position information from the sensor node attached to the object, and it transforms this to pan-tilt-zoom coodrinates for the camera, which will be described later.

- *The moving object* — this is an object marked with a visible marker and with an attached wireless node. A set of square shaped markers developed at Siemens Corporate Research Center [140] is used to mark each of the moving objects. An example of such a marker is shown in Figure 9.3. Visual markers are already widely used in many object tracking, motion tracking and pose estimation applications. Most commonly used markers are square shaped visual markers, since they provide at least 4 co-planar corresponding points that can be used for camera calibration. Further, every marker is determined by its unique ID number. Any type of marker can be used without

171

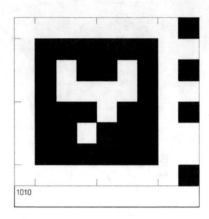

Figure 9.3: An example of the marker used in this system.

restriction with this system.

- *Central server* — this is a PC that collects the position data from the sensor node attached to the moving object, as well as the images obtained from the camera. The server runs the marker detection algorithm which, in case the marker of the object is captured on the image, extracts the information of the marker. There are many marker detection algorithms available based on the popular OpenCV library [141], any of which can be used here. In this project we have used the marker detection algorithm developed at Siemens Corporate Research [140].

9.3 Object Detection Through a WSN-based Positioning System

The moving object in this system has a wireless node attached, which continuously collects data about the received signal strength from the beacon nodes (given as the RSSI field in TinyOS packets), and based on this information it finds its position in the room. The estimated coordinates are labelled as (X_w, Y_w, Z_w), as shown in Figure 9.4. These coordinates, as well as the real coordinates of the object (X_m, Y_m, Z_m) are defined with respect to the reference coordinate system. Due to the propagation of the signal in an indoor environment,

172

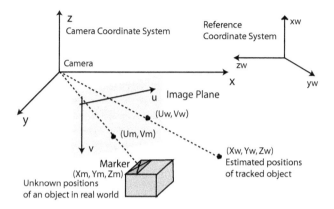

Figure 9.4: Scenario for high precision location system.

the RSSI value is actually a poor indicator of the received signal strength, which in most cases produces a difference between the estimated and the real coordinates of an object on the order of one meter or even more. Although roughly estimated, these coordinates can be used to point a camera in the proximity of the moving target. The coarse coordinates (X_w, Y_w, Z_w) are used as input information to the central server, which transforms them to the coordinates in the camera coordinate system, presented as the angle values of the camera (pan and tilt) and the camera's zoom parameter. The camera is then pointed toward the direction of the estimated coordinates (X_w, Y_w, Z_w). The camera continuously captures images from that area, and it sends them back to the central server. The server runs the marker detection algorithm, which processes the captured images and tries to detect the visible marker on the input images.

Depending on the size of the error between the estimated and the real values of the object's coordinates, two situations are likely to occur: either the marker attached to the object is within the camera's field of view and therefore captured on the image, or the marker is absent from the camera's field of view.

In the latter case, the system will not be able to improve the accuracy of the object's location provided by the set of beacon nodes during this update interval, and it has to wait for the next position information from the node attached to the tracked object. This update period is an adjustable parameter of the system, and its minimum value is equal to the period between two successful receptions of data packets from the node on the object. Since this period is on the order of a hundred milliseconds, we assume that this period does

173

not introduce large delays to the system. The camera continues to pan and tilt in this neighborhood until the object with the marker is detected as described below.

In the case when the marker is within the camera's field of view, the marker detection algorithm will detect the marker when analyzing the incoming image frames from the camera. In order to be detected from the image, every marker captured on an image by the camera should be of reasonable size (20×20 pixels at least). The marker detection algorithm provides the following information about every detected marker:

- four corners' coordinates of a marker (labelled as (x_1, y_1), (x_2, y_2), (x_3, y_3), (x_4, y_4))

- the coordinates of the middle point of a marker (labelled as (x_{middle}, y_{middle}))

- the unique ID number of the detected marker

In the following, we assume that the coordinates of the marker's middle point (x_{middle}, y_{middle}) correspond to the position of the object and thus should be estimated by this system.

In general, the marker detection algorithm is able to detect multiple markers from one image, in the case when more than one marked object is present (available) for tracking. In such situations, the positioning system is designed to provide precise positions of every object that has a detectable marker, assuming that every object is labelled with a different marker (which has a unique ID number). For the purpose of identifying each object based on the marker captured on an image, the system has a database in place, where the ID's of all moving sensor nodes (objects) and related markers are stored. The system repeats the algorithm for precise position estimation for every detected object.

In general, information from only one camera is not sufficient to detect complete information about the 3D location of a tracked object. The relationship between the coordinates of an object in 3D space and coordinates of the same object captured on the camera's image can be simply expressed by the transformation matrix [142]. This information, however, does not reveal any information about the "depth" or distance of this object from the camera, and we can only define a ray that passes from the camera through the object. Using at least two cameras that simultaneously capture the same object is sufficient to estimate the object's exact position, but this is more expensive in terms of hardware and communication cost.

174

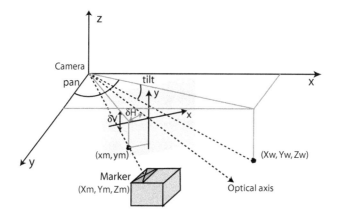

Figure 9.5: Estimation of the exact position of a tracked object.

9.4 Precise Object Localization Through Maker Detection

In our case, to localize the moving object with finer precision we have to find the distance between the marker attached to the object and the camera as well as the values of the horizontal and vertical angle of the object (δH and δV in Figure 9.5) by utilizing the marker's information obtained by only one camera.

First, note that the camera can detect the marker attached to an object without zooming only when the marker is close to the camera (on the order of 2-3 meters). In case the marker is further away, the camera has to zoom toward the marker in order to be able to detect it. When the camera zooms in, some intrinsic parameters such as the focal length of the camera change, which basically affects the size of the object (marker) captured on the image.

The variation in the size of the object's marker captured in the image for different values of the camera's ZOOM parameter is first examined. For this purpose the marker is placed normally at a distance of 1 meter from the camera, and we measured the length of one marker's edge, as the value of the ZOOM parameter linearly increases in the range [0, 1000]. The length of the marker's edge is measured in pixels on the image taken by the camera. As shown in Figure 9.6, for a linear increase in the ZOOM values, the length of the marker's edge changes in a nonlinear fashion.

Considering the format of the image provided by the camera (in this case, the images

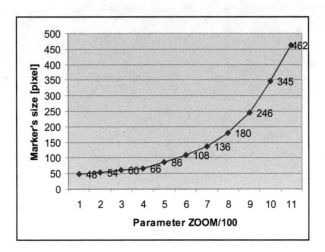

Figure 9.6: Change in marker's length with a change in ZOOM parameter.

were 640x480 pixels) and the full angle of the camera's field of view (angle that corresponds to the image when ZOOM = 0), we define the following camera parameter — the horizontal angle centered at the camera that corresponds to one pixel in the image plane (see Figure 9.7):

$$pixelAngle = \frac{\angle FOV}{imagewidth} \qquad \frac{rad}{pixel} \qquad (9.1)$$

The marker detection algorithm determines the coordinates of the marker's corners and the middle point with respect to the upper left corner of the image. For simplicity, we express the position of the marker's middle point with respect to the image coordinate system that is centered in the middle of the image plane:

$$x_m = \frac{imagewidth}{2} - x_{middle} \qquad (9.2)$$

$$y_m = \frac{imageheight}{2} - y_{middle} \qquad (9.3)$$

Given the pan and tilt angles of the camera, we calculate the horizontal ($angleH$) and vertical ($angleV$) angles of the middle marker's point (x_{middle}, y_{middle}) measured with respect to the camera's coordinate system. The parameter $angleH$ is measured in the same plane as the pan angle, and $angleV$ is measured in the same way as the tilt angle.

176

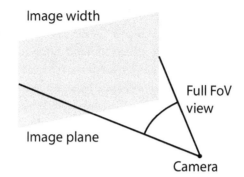

Figure 9.7: Calculation of the *pixelAngle* parameter.

From Figure 9.5 it can be seen that the horizontal angle ($angleH$) under which the marker's middle point is seen in the XY plane is equal to the value of the camera's pan angle plus angle δH measured between the camera's optical axis and the ray that passes through point $(x_m, 0)$. The δH angle can be simply found as:

$$\delta H = x_m \cdot pixelAngle \tag{9.4}$$

However, the camera's zoom has to be considered as well, since larger values of the camera's ZOOM parameter has the same effect as taking the image of an object from a smaller distance, which changes (makes bigger) the angle δH. Therefore, the angle δH has to be scaled to correspond to the horizontal angle taken for the case when ZOOM = 0:

$$\delta H(zoom = ZOOM) = \frac{x_m \cdot pixelAngle}{\frac{markerSize(zoom=ZOOM)}{markerSize(zoom=0)}} \tag{9.5}$$

The total horizontal angle is then:

$$angleH = PAN + \delta H \tag{9.6}$$

Similarly, the vertical angle can be calculated as:

$$\delta V(zoom = ZOOM) = \frac{y_m \cdot pixelAngle}{\frac{markerSize(zoom=ZOOM)}{markerSize(zoom=0)}} \tag{9.7}$$

$$angleV = TILT + \delta V \tag{9.8}$$

177

Thus, equations 9.6 and 9.8 completely determine the horizontal and vertical angles of the marker with respect to the camera coordinate system. In order to obtain the 3D coordinates of the tracked object, the distance from the camera to the marker has to be found. For the purpose of distance estimation, we use the coordinates of the marker's four corners that are detected earlier. First, we calculate the distance between any two adjacent corner points of the marker. By this, we get the lengths of the four edges of the marker. Then we take the length of the longest marker's edge as a reference distance:

$$refDistance = \max_{(i,j) \in EDGE} \sqrt{((x_i - x_j)^2 + (y_i - y_j)^2)} \tag{9.9}$$

This reference distance (size of marker's edge) is now used to determine the real distance of the marker from the camera. Given the fact that an object that is further away from the camera appears smaller on the image, and taking into account the zoom of the camera, the distance from the camera can be found as:

$$distance(marker, camera) = \frac{markerSize(zoom = ZOOM)}{refDistance} \tag{9.10}$$

Finally, the last step in the object localization involves transformation of the object's coordinates (given as $angleH$, $angleV$, $distance$) calculated in the camera coordinate system to a 3-dimensional Cartesian reference system. This step assumes that the position of the camera in the reference coordinate system is known and given as (X_c, Y_c, Z_c). Based on simple trigonometric calculations, the exact position of the object with respect to the reference coordinate system is found as:

$$X = X_c + distance(marker, camera) \cdot \sin(\pi - angleV) \cdot \sin(angleH) \tag{9.11}$$

$$Y = Y_c + distance(marker, camera) \cdot \sin(\pi - angleV) \cdot \cos(angleH) \tag{9.12}$$

$$Z = Z_c + distance(marker, camera) \cdot \cos(\pi - angleV) \tag{9.13}$$

9.5   Results

In this Section we present results showing estimated coordinates of an object obtained by the described system. We compare the estimated coordinates with the real coordinates of the tracked object, when the object is moving within a room of size 12 x 6 meters. In Figure 9.8

we plot the values of the estimated coordinates for every dimension (X, Y and Z) versus the real coordinates of the object, for the case when the object moves to different positions in the room. As shown in the figures, the difference between the values of the coordinates obtained by our camera-based position estimation system and the real values of the coordinates X, Y, and Z is not significant, and in most cases is at most a few tens of cm.

Figure 9.9 presents a snapshot of the distances estimated by the WSN-based positioning system. The system receives an update packet on the estimated coordinates from the node attached to the moving object every 200ms. The errors between the real and estimated distance of the object to the coordinate system were on the order of a few meters, which clearly demonstrates the advantage of a camera-based positioning system.

9.6 Summary

In this Chapter we described a system that estimates the locations of marked objects with high precision. The proposed system presents an enhancement of existing solutions for real-time positioning based on wireless sensor network technology. In existing systems for real-time positioning, a wireless sensor node estimates its position based on measurements of the received signal strength from static reference (beacon) nodes. Our solution utilizes the fusion of data obtained from sensor nodes and a camera. With the proposed system, the accuracy of the estimated positions of tracked objects can be drastically improved by an order of magnitude, which means that the error between the estimated positions and real positions of an asset is less than 50 cm. In the proposed solution, the object is required to carry a visible marker and it has a wireless sensor node attached that receives data from beacon nodes to determine a rough estimate of its position based on RSS.

The system presented here uses one camera, but the number of cameras in our system is not a limitation. Increasing the number of cameras increases the probability that the system can detect markers attached to the assets in a shorter period of time. However, it opens new questions related to the design and organization of such a system — for example, how to decide which camera is active at a certain moment, or which camera is responsible for detection and position estimation of some object.

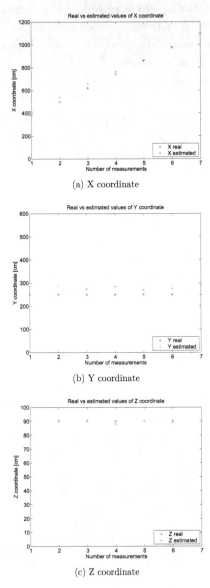

(a) X coordinate

(b) Y coordinate

(c) Z coordinate

Figure 9.8: Estimated values vs. real values for X, Y and Z coordinates of the moving object.

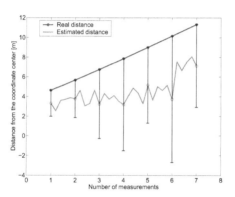

Figure 9.9: The error between the real distance of the object to the center of coordinate system and the distance estimated by the WSN-based positioning system.

Chapter 10

Conclusions and Future Work

In recent years we have witnessed an increasing number of sensor network applications, as a consequence of rapid progress in sensor networking technology that that is a result of recent developments in CMOS and MEMS technologies. However, battery technology is still not developing fast enough to follow the increasing needs of these new applications, so the problems of minimizing energy consumption in sensor networks will be present for the foreseeable future. Therefore, the main focus of this book is directed toward energy-efficient organization of sensor networks in a number of application-specific scenarios.

In Chapter 3 of this book we investigated the use of unequal size cluster-based sensor network architectures that provide balanced energy spending of the sensor nodes. Heterogeneous sensor networks are more sensitive to unbalanced energy consumption since the loss of the more important nodes (such as cluster head nodes) can lead to network partitioning and loss of data. Therefore, in these types of networks energy balancing is achieved by changing the sizes of clusters formed throughout the network. In homogeneous sensor networks energy balancing is additionally supported by rotating the cluster heads' roles among the nodes in the network.

Further analysis of sensor networks in different application-specific scenarios reveals that the importance of sensor nodes to the overall task is determined by the network's application. In Chapter 4 we analyzed this phenomena by looking into a cluster-based sensor network designed to provide maximized coverage over the monitored area. The nodes' importance to this particular task was defined through its application cost, which combines node energy constraints with the application QoS requirement (coverage, in this case) in an integrated manner. We concluded that such an integrated approach for characterizing the cost of the sensor nodes provides a better solution in terms of application QoS requirements – in this application, it provides longer coverage-time of the network.

We continued our work on application-specific resource balancing by concentrating on a specific type of sensor network – visual sensor networks.

Since the area of visual sensor networks is a relatively young research area, we started our work in this area by examining the problems common to wireless sensor networks in this type of network. In Chapter 6 we applied a routing protocol developed for wireless sensor networks to a visual sensor network. We showed that although both types of networks are constrained with the same resource limitations (in terms of energy) and with the same QoS requirements (in terms of coverage), there is no simple mapping of routing strategies from one type of network to the other.

In Chapter 7 we discussed methods for selecting camera-nodes in a visual sensor network. We started with a scenario when objects are not included in the scene, so that the problem is simplified to the coverage of planar scenes. We proposed several camera selection methods that provide the trade-off between a network lifetime and the quality of the reconstructed images. Finally, we provide input on how the camera selection problem can be approached in the case when objects appear in the monitored scene.

Further analysis of resource utilization in visual sensor networks was performed in Chapter 8, where we discussed the camera scheduling problem. Considering the energy constraints of the camera-nodes, we developed a camera scheduling model, where in every instance of time only a subset of the cameras is active. We provided directions for how multiple user queries can be merged in order to serve them in a minimum time.

In Chapter 9 we described the implementation of a localization system that provides the coordinates of a sensor nodes with fine precision by fusing the location information obtained from sensor nodes and position information obtained from images.

10.1   Future Work

In the first part of this book, we presented guidelines for the design and management of wireless sensor networks. This work is simulation-based. However, many factors, such as environmental conditions, unreliable wireless channels or sensor node imperfections will affect the performance of real sensor network. Recently, the research in wireless sensor networks has started to be evaluated by implementing the communication protocols on real sensor network test-beds. Further development of large scale test-beds will enable the comprehensive testing of a sensor network's scalability, and it will validate the communication protocols developed so far. Considering this, the next step is to implement and test the behavior of our proposed cluster-based architectures for balancing energy and preserving coverage.

Application-aware cost metrics used throughout this book for the sensor nodes' roles assignment assume that the exact positions of sensor nodes are known. In the case when the location estimation error is comparable with the nodes' sensing range, this error can produce the inaccurate estimation of nodes' cost metrics. Thus, our future work will be directed toward exploring the impact of inaccurate location estimate on the application cost-based approach for sensor management in wireless sensor networks.

In this book we analyzed several problems in a specific user-centric application of visual sensor networks, namely remote tele-presence. Since in this application the user determines which portion of the monitored area is of interest, all decisions related to network management (such as selection of cameras, camera scheduling for data transmission, etc.) are determined at a central server. This design is a consequence of the harsh constraints placed on the system by the limited network resources and the application requirements. A more generic approach for the design of visual sensor networks can be developed considering a broad range of possible applications of visual sensor networks.

The design and resource utilization in a user-centric visual sensor network is constrained in several ways. First, there is the constant requirement for the reduction of energy consumption – this problem was addressed several times throughout this book. Also, the maximum achievable data rate is limited by the commonly used IEEE 802.15.4 standard, but this data rate is insufficient to obtain image data in real-time. One solution to this problem would be to use radios with higher data rates, such as those that support IEEE 802.11g or IEEE 802.11n, but this comes at the cost of increasing the energy consumption as well as the price of the camera-nodes devices.

Further improvements in in camera-node hardware design introduce new possibilities for optimizing the performance of application-specific visual sensor networks. In this book we assume that camera-nodes have only small data storage that is incapable of holding one image frame. However, if the camera-node is equipped with enough memory to store at least one image, the sensor node can perform more complex processing tasks on board, before the data is transmitted. For example, the node can decide if the captured image data is "worth" transmitting or not. For this, the sensor nodes can apply simple background substraction of the captured image from the previous image stored in the memory. Also, having more memory space enables sensor nodes to perform on board image compression, further reducing the transmitting load.

Future research should focus on higher-level on-board processing of the image data. For example, based on the content of the captured image a sensor node could determine appropriate compression gains for different parts of the image. For example, if the basic task of the visual network is to capture and track a target, then, depending on whether or not a sensor node views a target, it can separate the less relevant image parts from the image of the target and compress the less relevant image parts with higher compression gain.

Although in this work we provided an analysis of network lifetime and image quality, we did not explicitly consider the relationship between the resolution of the captured images and the achievable resolution of the final reconstructed image. A camera can capture images of some arbitrary scene/object either from a larger distance (thereby covering a lager portion of the scene with low resolution) or from a smaller distance to the scene/object (providing thereby a high resolution image while capturing a smaller part of the scene). Therefore, this work can be further extended by looking into the trade-offs obtained using different numbers of cameras and images with different resolution in order to obtain multi-resolution reconstructed images.

As we conclude this book, we would like to point out that visual sensor networks will continue to attract much attention as a new type of surveillance network with the ability to reason intelligently based on captured images. Thus, the main trend in the development of new camera-node architectures is to support embedded processing and higher level reasoning. Therefore, future work on protocols and algorithms for visual sensor networks should be aimed at exploiting these new features to provide further benefit to visual sensor networks.

Bibliography

[1] D. Yang, H. Gonzalez-Banos, and L. Guibas, "Counting people in crowds with a real-time network of image sensors," in *Proceedings of the 9th IEEE International Conference on Computer Vision*, 2003.

[2] S. Soro and W. Heinzelman, "On the coverage problem in video-based wireless sensor networks," in *Proceedings of the Second Workshop on Broadband Advanced Sensor Networks (BaseNets '05)*, 2005.

[3] A. Rowe, D. Goel, and R. Rajkumar, "FireFly Mosaic: A vision-enabled wireless sensor networking system," in *Proceedings of 28th IEEE International Real-Time Systems Symposium (RTSS)*, 2007.

[4] T. S. Rappaport, *Wireless Communications, Principle and Practice.* IEEE Press, Prentice Hall, 1996.

[5] A. Ghosh, D. R. Wolter, J. G. Andrews, and R. Chen, "Broadband wireless access with WiMax/IEEE 802.16: Current performance benchmarks and future potential," *IEEE Communications Magazine*, vol. 43, pp. 129–136, Feb 2005.

[6] T. Cooklev, *Wireless Communications Standards: A Study of IEEE 802.11, 802.15, and 802.16.* IEEE Press, Standards Information Network, 2004.

[7] S. Basagni, M. Conti, S. Giordano, and I. Stojmenović, *Mobile Ad hoc Networking.* John Wiley & Sons, 2004.

[8] IEEE Computer Society (LAN MAN) Standards Committee, *Wireless LAN Medium Access Control (MAC) and Physical Layer (PHY) Specifications*, 1999.

[9] C. Raghavendra, K. Sivalingam, and T. Znati, *Wireless Sensor Networks: An Information Processing Approach.* Morgan Kaufmann Publishers, 2004.

[10] V. Raghunathan, C. Schurgers, and M. Shrivastava, "Energy-aware wireless microsensor networks," *IEEE Signal Processing Magazine*, vol. 19, pp. 40–50, March 2002.

[11] N. Sadagopan and B. Krishnamachari, "Maximizing data extraction in energy-limited sensor networks," in *Proceedings of the Twenty Third Annual Joint Conference of the IEEE Computer and Communications Societies (INFOCOM)*, 2004.

[12] G. J. Pottie and W. J. Kaiser, "Wireless integrated network sensors," *ACM Communications*, vol. 43, pp. 51–58, May 2000.

[13] A. Goldsmith, *Wireless Communications*. Cambridge University Press, 2005.

[14] S. Pattem, B. Krishnamachari, and R. Govindan, "The impact of spatial correlation on routing with compression in wireless sensor networks," in *Proceedings of the Third International Symposium on Information Processing in Sensor Networks (IPSN)*, 2004.

[15] D. Chen and P. K. Varshney, "Qos support in wireless sensor networks: A survey," in *Proc. of the 2004 International Conference on Wireless Networks (ICWN 2004), Las Vegas, Nevada, USA*, 2004.

[16] M. Cardei, I. Cardei, and D.-Z. Du, *Resource Management in Wireless Networking (Network Theory and Applications)*. Springer-Verlag New York, Inc., 2006. chapter: QoS for Multimedia Services in Wireless Networks.

[17] W. Heinzelman, A. Chandrakasan, and H.Balakrishnan, "An application specific protocol architecture for wireless microsensor networks," *IEEE Transactions on Wireless Communications*, vol. 1, pp. 660–670, Oct 2002.

[18] O. Younis and S. Fahmy, "HEED: A hybrid, energy-efficient, distributed clustering approach for ad-hoc sensor networks," *IEEE Transactions on Mobile Computing*, vol. 3, pp. 366–379, Oct-Dec 2004.

[19] M. Chatterjee, S. K. Das, and D. Turgut, "WCA: A weighted clustering algorithm for mobile ad hoc networks," *Cluster Computing*, vol. 5, pp. 193–204, Apr 2002.

[20] S. Bandyopadhyay and E. J. Coyle, "An energy efficient hierarchical clustering algorithm for wireless sensor networks," in *Proceedings of the 22nd Annual Joint Conference of the IEEE Computer and Communications Societies*, 2003.

[21] H. Chan and A. Perrig, "ACE: An emergent algorithm for highly uniform cluster formation," in *Proceedings of European Workshop on Sensor Networks (EWSN)*, 2004.

[22] http://ubimon.doc.ic.ac.uk/bsn/index.php?m=206. Overview of current sensor node platforms.

[23] I. F. Akyildiz, W. Su, Y. Sankarasubramaniam, and E. Cayirci, "A survey on sensor networks," *IEEE Communications Magazine*, vol. 42, pp. 102–114, Aug. 2002.

[24] W. Ye, J. Heidemann, and D. Estrin, "An energy-efficient MAC protocol for wireless sensor networks," in *Proceedings of Twenty-First Annual Joint Conference of the IEEE Computer and Communications Societies (INFOCOM)*, 2002.

[25] J. Polastre, J. Hill, and D. Culler, "Versatile low power media access for wireless sensor networks," in *Proceedings of the 2nd International Conference on Embedded Networked Sensor Systems (SenSys)*, 2004.

[26] M. Buettner, G. V. Yee, E. Anderson, and R. Han, "X-MAC: a short preamble MAC protocol for duty-cycled wireless sensor networks," in *Proceedings of the 4th ACM International Conference on Embedded Networked Sensor Systems (SenSys)*, 2006.

[27] I. Rhee, A. Warrier, M. Aia, and J. Min, "Z-MAC: a hybrid MAC for wireless sensor networks," in *Proceedings of the 3rd ACM International Conference on Embedded Networked Sensor Systems (SenSys)*, 2005.

[28] J. Kulik, W. Heinzelman, and H. Balakrishnan, "Negotiation-based protocols for disseminating information in wireless sensor networks," *Wireless Networks*, vol. 8, no. 2-3, pp. 169–185, 2002.

[29] C. Intanagonwiwat, R. Govindan, and D. Estrin, "Directed diffusion: a scalable and robust communication paradigm for sensor networks," in *Proceedings of the 6th Annual ACM/IEEE International Conference on Mobile Computing and Networking (MobiCom)*, 2000.

[30] D. Culler, P. Dutta, C. Ee, R. Fonseca, J. Hui, P. Levis, J. Polastre, S. Shenker, I. Stoica, G. Tolle, and J. Zhao, "Towards a sensor network architecture: Lowering the waistline," in *Proceedings of Hot Topics in Operating Systems (HotOS X)*, 2005.

[31] A. Mainwaring, J. Polastre, R. Szewczyk, and D. Culler, "Wireless sensor networks for habitat monitoring," in *Proceedings of the 1st ACM International Workshop on Wireless Sensor Networks and Applications*, 2002.

[32] K. Lorincz, D. Malan, T. Fulford-Jones, A. Nawoj, A. Clavel, V. Shnayder, G. Mainland, S. Moulton, and M. Welsh, "Sensor networks for emergency response: Challenges and opportunities," *IEEE Pervasive Computing*, vol. 3, pp. 16–23, Oct.-Dec. 2004.

[33] J. Polastre, R. Szewczyk, and D. Culler, "Telos: Enabling ultra-low power wireless research," in *Proceedings of the 4th International Symposium on Information Processing in Sensor Networks (IPSN)*, 2005.

[34] A. Wang, S.-H. Cho, C. Godini, and A. Chandrakasan, "Energy-efficient modulation and MAC for asymmetric microsensor systems," in *Proceedings of International Symposium on Low Power Electronic Devices and Design*, 2001.

[35] J. Polastre, R. Szewczyk, C. Sharp, and D. Culler, "The mote revolution: Low power wireless sensor network devices," in *Proceedings of Hot Chips: A Symposium on High Performance Chips*, 2004.

[36] C. Raghavendra, K. Sivalingam, and T. Znati, *Wireless Sensor Networks*. Kluwer Academic Publishers, 2004.

[37] S. Singh, M. Woo, and C. S. Raghavendra, "Power-aware routing in mobile ad hoc networks," in *Proccedings of IEEE/ACM International Conference on Mobile Computing and Networking (MobiCom)*, 1998.

[38] J.H.Chang and L.Tassiulas, "Routing for maximum system lifetime in wireless ad-hoc networks," in *Proceedings of 37th Annual Allerton Conference on Communication, Control and Computation*, 1999.

[39] C. Toh, H. Cobb, and D. Scott, "Performance evaluation of battery-life-aware routing optimization schemes for wireless ad hoc networks," in *Proceedings of IEEE International Computing Conference*, 2001.

[40] Q. Li, J. Aslam, and D. Rus, "Online power-aware routing in wireless ad-hoc networks," in *Proceedings of ACM/IEEE International Conference on Mobile Computing and Networking (MobiCom)*, 2001.

189

[41] W. R. Heinzelman, J. Kulik, and H. Balakrishnan, "Adaptive protocols for information dissemination in wireless sensor networks," in *Proceedings of the 5th Annual ACM/IEEE International Conference on Mobile Computing and Networking (MobiCom)*, 1999.

[42] S. Misra, M. Reisslein, and G. Xue, "A survey of multimedia streaming in wireless sensor networks," in *technical report, Dept. of Electrical Engineering, Arizona State University*, 2006.

[43] T. He, J. A. Stankovic, C. Lu, and T. F. Abdelzaher, "SPEED: A stateless protocol for real-time communication in sensor networks," in *Proceedings of the 23rd International Conference on Distributed Computing Systems*, 2003.

[44] M. Perillo and W. Heinzelman, "DAPR: A protocol for wireless sensor networks utilizing an application-based routing cost," in *Proceedings of the IEEE Wireless Communications and Networking Conference (WCNC)*, 2004.

[45] J. Deng, Y. Han, W. Heinzelman, and P. Varshney, "Scheduling sleeping nodes in high density cluster-based sensor networks," *ACM/Kluwer MONET Special Issue on Energy Constraints and Lifetime Performance in Wireless Sensor Networks*, vol. 10, pp. 825–835, Dec 2005.

[46] J. Deng, Y. Han, W. Heinzelman, and P. Varsney, "Balanced-energy sleep scheduling scheme for high density cluster-based sensor networks," *Elsevier's Computer Communications Journal*, vol. 28, pp. 1631–1642, 2005.

[47] V. Mhatre and C. Rosenberg, "Homogeneous vs. heterogeneous clustered networks: a comparative study," in *Proceedings of IEEE International Conference on Communications (ICC)*, 2004.

[48] G. Smaragdakis, I. Matta, and A. Bestavros, "SEP: a stable election protocol for clustered heterogeneous wireless sensor networks," in *Proceedings of 2nd International Workshop on Sensor and Actor Network Protocols and Applications*, 2004.

[49] X. Wang, G. Xing, Y. Zhang, C. Lu, R. Pless, and C. Gill, "Integrated coverage and connectivity configuration in wireless sensor networks," in *Proceedings of the 1st ACM Conference on Embedded Networked Sensor Systems (SenSys)*, 2003.

[50] Z. Zhou, S. Das, and H. Gupta, "Connected k-coverage problem in sensor networks," in *Proceedings of 13th International Conference on Computer Communications and Networks*, 2004.

[51] M. Bhardwaj and A. Chandrakasan, "Bounding the lifetime of sensor networks via optimal role assignments," in *Proceedings of Proceedings of 21th Annual Joint Conference of the IEEE Computer and Communications Societies (INFOCOM)*, 2002.

[52] M. Cardei and J. Wu, "Energy-efficient coverage problems in wireless ad hoc sensor networks," *Computer Communications Journal (Elsevier)*, vol. 29, pp. 413–420, Feb. 2006.

[53] D. Tian and N. Georganas, "A coverage-preserving node scheduling scheme for large wireless sensor networks," in *Proceedings of the 1st ACM Workshop on Wireless Sensor Networks and Applications*, 2002.

[54] B. Chen, K. Jamieson, H. Balakrishnan, and R. Morris, "SPAN: An energy-efficient coordination algorithm for topology maintenance in ad hoc wireless networks," in *Proceedings of ACM/IEEE International Conference on Mobile Computing and Networking (MobiCom)*, 2001.

[55] F. Ye, G. Zhong, J. Cheng, S. Lu, and L. Zhang, "PEAS: A robust energy conserving protocol for long-lived sensor networks," in *Proceedings of International Conference on Distributed Computing Systems*, 2003.

[56] H. Zhang and J. Hou, "Maintaining coverage and connectivity in large sensor networks," in *Proceedings of International Workshop on Theoretical and Algorithmic Aspects of Sensor, Ad hoc Wireless and Peer-to-Peer Networks*, 2004.

[57] S. Soro and W. Heinzelman, "Prolonging the lifetime of wireless sensor networks via unequal clustering," in *Proceedings of the 5th International Workshop on Algorithms for Wireless, Mobile, Ad Hoc and Sensor Networks (IEEE WMAN '05)*, 2005.

[58] http://mathworld.wolfram.com/CircularSector.html. Finding a Centroid of a Circular Sector.

[59] S. Soro and W. Heinzelman, "Cluster head election techniques for coverage preservation in wireless sensor networks," *Elsevier Ad Hoc Networks Journal*, 2009. , in press.

191

[60] M. Handy, M. Haase, and D. Timmermann, "Low energy adaptive clustering hierarchy with deterministic cluster head selection," in *Proceedings of IEEE International Conference on Mobile and Wireless Communications Networks(IEEE MWCN)*, 2002.

[61] W. Choi and S. K. Das, "A framework for energy-saving data gathering using two-phase clustering in wireless sensor networks," in *Proceedings of the 1st Annual International Conference on Mobile and Ubiquitous Systems (MOBIQUITOUS)*, 2004.

[62] M. Qin and R. Zimmermann, "An energy-efficient voting-based clustering algorithm for sensor networks," in *Proceedings of the 6th International Conference on Software Engineering, Artificial Intelligence, Networking and Parallel/Distributed Computing*, 2005.

[63] T. Shu, M. Krunz, and S. Vrudhula, "Power balanced coverage-time optimization for clustered wireless sensor networks," in *Proceedings of the 6th ACM International Symposium on Mobile Ad Hoc Networking and Computing (MobiHoc)*, 2005.

[64] S. Meguerdichian, F. Koushanfar, M. Potkonjak, and M. Srivastava, "Coverage problems in wireless ad-hoc sensor networks," in *Proceedings of Proceedings of 20th Annual Joint Conference of the IEEE Computer and Communications Societies (INFOCOM)*, 2001.

[65] R. C. Gonzales and R. E. Woods, *Digital Image Processing*. Addison-Wesley Publishing Company, 1992.

[66] R. Hartley and A. Zisserman, *Multiple View Geometry in Computer Vision*. Cambridge University Press, 2000.

[67] S. Hengstler, D. Prashanth, S. Fong, and H. Aghajan, "Mesheye: A hybrid-resolution smart camera mote for applications in distributed intelligent surveillance," in *Proceedings of Information Processing in Sensor Networks (IPSN-SPOTS)*, 2007.

[68] W. Wolf, B. Ozer, and T. Lv, "Smart cameras as embedded systems," *IEEE Computer*, vol. 35, pp. 48–53, Sept. 2002.

[69] M. Wu and C. W. Chen, "Multiple bitstream image transmission over wireless sensor networks," *IEEE Sensors*, vol. 2, pp. 727–731, Oct. 2003.

[70] K. Römer, P. Blum, and L. Meier, "Time synchronization and calibration in wireless sensor networks," in *Handbook of Sensor Networks: Algorithms and Architectures* (I. Stojmenović, ed.), pp. 199–237, John Wiley and Sons, Sept. 2005.

[71] P. Remagnino, A. I. Shihab, and G. A. Jones, "Distributed intelligence for multi-camera visual surveillance," *Pattern Recognition*, vol. 37, no. 4, pp. 675–689, 2004.

[72] T. He, S. Krishnamurthy, L. Luo, T. Yan, L. Gu, R. Stoleru, G. Zhou, Q. Cao, P. Vicaire, J. A. Stankovic, T. F. Abdelzaher, J. Hui, and B. Krogh, "Vigilnet: An integrated sensor network system for energy-efficient surveillance," *ACM Transaction on Sensor Networks*, vol. 2, no. 1, pp. 1–38, 2006.

[73] O. Schreer, P. Kauff, and T. Sikora, *3D Video Communication*. John Willey & Sons, 2005.

[74] N. J. McCurdy and W. Griswold, "A system architecture for ubiquitous video," in *Proceedings of Mobysis*, 2005.

[75] S. Hengstler and H. Aghajan, "Application-oriented design of smart camera networks," in *Proceedings of 1st International Conference on Distributed Smart Cameras (ICDSC)*, 2007.

[76] A. Barton-Sweeney, D. Lymberopoulos, and A. Savvides, "Sensor localization and camera calibration in distributed camera sensor networks," in *Proceedings of IEEE BaseNets*, 2006.

[77] S. Funiak, C. Guestrin, M. Paskin, and R. Sukthankar, "Distributed localization of networked cameras," in *Proceedings of 5th International Symposium on Information Processing in Sensor Networks (IPSN)*, 2006.

[78] C. Taylor, "A scheme for calibrating smart camera networks using active lights," in *Proceedings of ACM SenSys*, 2004.

[79] D. Devarajan, R. J. Radke, and H. Chung, "Distributed metric calibration of ad-hoc camera networks," *ACM Transactions on Sensor Networks*, vol. 2, pp. 380–403, Aug. 2006.

[80] D. Yang, J. Shin, A. Ercan, , and L. Guibas, "Sensor tasking for occupancy reasoning in a network of cameras," in *Proceedings of IEEE 2nd International Conference on Broadband Communications, Networks and Systems (BaseNets)*, 2004.

[81] A. Lipton, H. Fujiyoshi, and R. Patil, "Moving target classification and tracking from real-time video," in *Proceedings of IEEE Image Understanding Workshop*, 1998.

[82] P. Pahalawatta, T. Pappas, and A. Katsaggelos, "Optimal sensor selection for video-based target tracking in a wireless sensor network," in *Proceedings of IEEE International Conference on Image Processing*, 2004.

[83] S. Fleck, F. Busch, , and W. Straer, "Adaptive probabilistic tracking embedded in smart cameras for distributed surveillance in a 3d model," *EURASIP Journal on Embedded Systems*, vol. 2007, 2007. Article ID 29858.

[84] F. Lau, E. Oto, and H. Aghajan, "Color-based multiple agent tracking for wireless image sensor networks," in *Proceedings of Advanced Concepts for Intelligent Vision Systems (ACIVS)*, 2006.

[85] T. H. Ko and N. M. Berry, "On scaling distributed low-power wireless image sensors," in *Proceedings of the 39th Hawaii International Conference on System Sciences*, 2006.

[86] A. Ercan, A. E. Gamal, and L. Guibas, "Camera network node selection for target localization in the presence of occlusions," in *Proceedings of ACM SenSys Workshop on Distributed Smart Cameras*, 2006.

[87] T. Teixeira, D. Lymberopoulos, E. Culurciello, Y. Aloimonos, and A. Savvides, "A lightweight camera sensor network operating on symbolic information," in *Proceedings of First Workshop on Distributed Smart Cameras, held in conjunction with ACM SenSys*, 2006.

[88] H. Aghajan and C. Wu, "From distributed vision networks to human behavior interpretation," in *Proceedings of Behaviour Monitoring and Interpretation Workshop at the 30th German Conference on Artificial Intelligence*, 2007.

[89] J. Dagher, M. Marcellin, and M. Neifeld, "A method for coordinating the distributed transmission of imagery," *IEEE Transactions on Image Processing*, vol. 15, pp. 1705–1717, July 2006.

[90] J. Park, P. Bhat, and A. Kak, "A look-up table based approach for solving the camera selection problem in large camera networks," in *Proceedings of the International Workshop on Distributed Smart Cameras*, 2006.

[91] S. Soro and W. Heinzelman, "Camera selection in visual sensor networks," in *Proceedings of IEEE International Conference on Advanced Video and Signal based Surveillance (AVSS)*, 2007.

[92] N. H. Zamora and R. Marculescu, "Coordinated distributed power management with video sensor networks: Analysis, simulation, and prototyping," in *Proceedings of the 1st ACM/IEEE International Conference on Distributed Smart Cameras*, 2007.

[93] Z. Yang and K. Nahrstedt, "A bandwidth management framework for wireless camera array," in *Proceedings of International Workshop on Network and Operating Systems Support for Digital Audio and Video (NOSSDAV)*, 2005.

[94] M. Chen, V. Leung, S. Mao, and Y. Yuan, "DGR: Directional geographical routing for real-time video communications in wireless sensor networks," *Computer Communications, Special Issue On Concurrent Multipath Transfer*, vol. 30, pp. 3368–3383, Nov. 2007.

[95] E. Felemban, L. Chang-Gun, and E. Ekici, "Mmspeed: multipath multi-speed protocol for qos guarantee of reliability and timeliness in wireless sensor networks," *IEEE Transactions on Mobile Computing*, vol. 5, pp. 738–754, June 2006.

[96] K. Obraczka, R. Manduchi, and J. Garcia-Luna-Aveces, "Managing the information flow in visual sensor networks," in *Proceedings of the 5th International Symposium on Wireless Personal Multimedia Communications*, 2002.

[97] H. Medeiros, J. Park, and A. C. Kak, "A light-weight event-driven protocol for sensor clustering in wireless camera networks," in *Proceedings of the 1st ACM/IEEE International Conference on Distributed Smart Cameras*, 2007.

[98] H. Zhang and J. C. Hou, "Maintaining sensing coverage and connectivity in large sensor networks," *International Journal of Wireless Ad Hoc and Sensor Networks*, vol. 1, no. 2, pp. 89–124, 2005.

[99] S. Hengstler and H. Aghajan, "WiSNAP: A wireless image sensor network application platform," in *Proceedings of 2nd International Conference on Testbeds and Research Infrastructures for the Development of Networks and Communities (TridentCom)*, 2006.

[100] M. Rahimi, R. Baer, O. I. Iroezi, J. C. Garcia, J. Warrior, D. Estrin, and M. Srivastava, "Cyclops: in situ image sensing and interpretation in wireless sensor networks,"

in *Proceedings of the 3rd International Conference on Embedded Networked Sensor Systems*, 2005.

[101] W. Feng, B. Code, E. Kaiser, M. Shea, W. Feng, and L. Bavoil, "Panoptes: a scalable architecture for video sensor networking applications," in *Proceedings of ACM Multimedia*, 2003.

[102] C. B. Margi, R. Manduchi, and K. Obraczka, "Energy consumption tradeoffs in visual sensor networks," in *Proceedings of 24th Brazilian Symposium on Computer Networks (SBRC)*, 2006.

[103] `http://www.xbow.com/Products/productdetails.aspx?sid=229`. Stargate gateway sensor board.

[104] D. Jung, T. Texeira, A. Barton-Sweeney, and A. Savvides, "Model-based design exploration of wireless sensor node lifetimes," in *Proceedings of the 4th European Conference on Wireless Sensor Networks*, 2007.

[105] `http://www.intel.com/research/exploratory/motes.htm`. Intel iMote wireless sensor node platform.

[106] L. Ferrigno, S. Marano, V. Paciello, and A. Pietrosanto, "Balancing computational and transmission power consumption in wireless image sensor networks," in *IEEE International Conference on Virtual Environments, Human-Computer Interfaces and Measurement Systems*, 2005.

[107] `http://www.xbow.com/Products/Product\_pdf\_files/Wireless\_pdf/MICA2\_Datasheet.pdf`. Mica2 wireless sensor node.

[108] R. Kleihorst, B. Schueler, A. Danilin, and M. Heijligers, "Smart camera mote with high performance vision system," in *Proceedings of ACM SenSys 2006 Workshop on Distributed Smart Cameras*, 2006.

[109] A. Rowe, A. Goode, D. Goel, and I. Nourbakhsh, "CMUcam3: An open programmable embedded vision sensor," Tech. Rep. RI-TR-07-13, Carnegie Mellon Robotics Institute, 2007.

[110] IEEE Computer Society LAN MAN Standards Committee, *Wireless Medium Access Control (MAC) and Physical Layer (PHY) Specifications for Low Rate Wireless Personal Area Networks (LR-WPANs)*, 2003.

[111] P. Kulkarni, D. Ganesan, P. Shenoy, and Q. Lu, "SensEye: A multi-tier camera sensor network," in *Proceedings of ACM Multimedia*, 2005.

[112] http://www.xbow.com. Crossbow Teachnology, Inc.

[113] A. Rowe, R. Mangharam, and R. Rajkumar, "Rt-link: A time-synchronized link protocol for energy constrained multi-hop wireless networks," in *Proceedings of IEEE Communications Society Conference on Sensor, Mesh and Ad Hoc Communications and Networks (SECON)*, 2006.

[114] M. Molla and S. Ahamed, "A survey of middleware for sensor network and challenges," in *Proceedings of IEEE International Conference on Parallel Processing Workshops*, 2006.

[115] B. Rinner, M. Jovanovic, and M. Quaritsch, "Embedded middleware on distributed smart cameras," in *Proceedings of IEEE International Conference on Acoustics, Speech and Signal Processing*, 2007.

[116] H. Detmold, A. Dick, K. Falkner, D. Munro, A. van den Hengel, and R. Morrison, "Middleware for video surveillance networks," in *Proceedings of Middleware for Sensor Networks (MidSens)*, 2006.

[117] Z. Xiong, A. Liveris, and S. Cheng, "Distributed source coding for sensor networks," *IEEE Signal Processing Magazine*, vol. 21, pp. 80–94, 2004.

[118] S. Meyer and A. Rakotonirainy, "A survey of research on context-aware homes," in *Proceedings of the Australasian Information Security Workshop Conference on ACSW Frontiers*, Australian Computer Society, Inc., 2003.

[119] C. Huang, Y.Tseng, and L. Lo, "The coverage problem in three dimensional wireless sensor networks," in *Proceedings of IEEE Global Telecommunications Conference (GLOBECOM)*, 2004.

[120] L. Zhong, J. M. Rabaey, and A. Wolisz, "Does proper coding make single hop wireless networks reality: the power consumption perspective," in *Proceedings of the IEEE Wireless Communications and Networking Conference (WCNC)*, 2005.

[121] C. Yu, S. Soro, G. Sharma, and W. Hinzelman, "Lifetime-distortion trade-off in image sensor networks," in *Proceedings of IEEE International Conference on Image Processing (ICIP)*, 2007.

[122] S. Soro and W. Hinzelman, "Camera selection in visual sensor networks with occluding objects," in *Proceedings of ACM/IEEE 1st International Conference on Distributed and Smart Cameras (ICDSC)*, 2007.

[123] S. Slijepcevic and M. Potkonjak, "Power efficient organization of wireless sensor networks," in *Proceedings of the IEEE International Conference on Communications*, 2001.

[124] M. Cardei, M. Thai, Y. Li, and W. Wu, "Energy-efficient target coverage in wireless sensor networks," in *Proceedings of the IEEE INFOCOM*, 2005.

[125] P. Berman, G. Calinescu, C. Shah, and A. Zelikovsky, "Power efficient monitoring management in sensor networks," in *Proceedings of IEEE Wireless Communication and Networking Conference (WCNC)*, 2004.

[126] N. Garg and J. Könemann, "Faster and simpler algorithms for multicommodity flow and other fractional packing problems," in *IEEE Symposium on Foundations of Computer Science*, pp. 300–309, 1998.

[127] `http://www.kodak.com/ezpres/business/ccd/global/plugins/acrobat/en/productsummary/CMOS/KAC-5000ProductSummaryv1.0.pdf`. Kodak KAC-5000 Image Sensor.

[128] `http://www.ovt.com`. Omnivision Technologies, Inc.

[129] N. Patwari, J. N. Ash, S. Kyperountas, A. O. Hero, R. L. Moses, and N. S. Correal, "Locating the nodes: cooperative localization in wireless sensor networks," *Signal Processing Magazine, IEEE*, vol. 22, no. 4, pp. 54–69, 2005.

[130] A. Savvides, C. C. Han, and M. B. Strivastava, "Dynamic fine-grained localization in ad-hoc networks of sensors," in *Proceedings of ACM/IEEE International Conference on Mobile Computing and Networking (MobiCom)*, 2001.

[131] S. Pace, G. Frost, I. Lachow, D. Frelinger, D. Fossum, D. K.Wassem, and M. Pinto, "The Global Positioning System – history, chronology and budgets," in *RAND Corporation*, 1995.

[132] C. Savarese, J. Rabaey, and J. Beutel, "Locationing in distributed ad-hoc wireless sensor networks," in *Proceedings of International Conference on Acoustics, Speech and Signal Processing*, 2001.

[133] N. Priyantha, A. Miu, H. Balakrishnan, and S. Teller, "The cricket compass for context-aware mobile applications," in *Proceedings of ACM/IEEE 7th International Conference on Mobile Computing and Networking*, 2001.

[134] J. Hightower, C. Vakili, G. Borriello, and R. Want, "Design and calibration of the spoton ad-hoc location sensing system," tech. rep., 2001.

[135] K. Lorincz and M. Welsh, "Motetrack: a robust, decentralized approach to rf-based location tracking," in *Proceedings of the International Workshop on Location and Context-Awareness (LoCA)*, 2005.

[136] C. Shen, B. Wang, F. Vogt, S. Oldridge, and S. Fels, "Remoteeyes: a remote low-cost position sensing infrastructure for ubiquitous computing," in *Proceedings of 1st International Workshop on Networked Sensing Systems*, 2004.

[137] J. Krumm, S. Harris, B. Meyers, B. Brumitt, M. Hale, and S. Shafer, "Multi-camera multi-person tracking for easy living," in *Proceedings of the 3rd IEEE International Workshop on Visual Surveillance*, 2000.

[138] S. Soro, M. Faschinger, C. Sastry, and Y. Genc, "Precise asset tracking through fusion of coarse location information from a wireless sensor network and video imagery from a camera," in *Technical Report, Siemens Corporate Research*, 2006.

[139] http://www.moteiv.com/products-tmotesky.php. Moteiv, Tmote Sky node platform.

[140] X. Zhang, S. Fronz, and N. Navab, "Visual marker detection and decoding in ar systems: A comparative study," in *Proceedings of the International Symposium on Mixed and Augmented Reality (ISMAR)*, 2002.

[141] http://sourceforge.net/projects/opencv/. Open Computer Vision Library.

[142] A. Tekalp, *Digital Video Processing*. Prentice Hall Signal Processing Series, 1995.

Wissenschaftlicher Buchverlag bietet

kostenfreie

Publikation

von

wissenschaftlichen Arbeiten

Diplomarbeiten, Magisterarbeiten, Master und Bachelor Theses
sowie Dissertationen, Habilitationen und wissenschaftliche Monographien

Sie verfügen über eine wissenschaftliche Abschlußarbeit zu aktuellen oder zeitlosen
Fragestellungen, die hohen inhaltlichen und formalen Ansprüchen genügt,
und haben **Interesse an einer honorarvergüteten Publikation**?

Dann senden Sie bitte erste Informationen über Ihre Arbeit per Email
an info@vdm-verlag.de. Unser Außenlektorat meldet sich umgehend bei Ihnen.

VDM Verlag Dr. Müller Aktiengesellschaft & Co. KG
Dudweiler Landstraße 125a
D - 66123 Saarbrücken

www.vdm-verlag.de

www.ingramcontent.com/pod-product-compliance
Lightning Source LLC
LaVergne TN
LVHW022310060326
832902LV00020B/3381